Presenting
THE
PHILIPPINES

This edition first published in the United Kingdom in 2012
by John Beaufoy Publishing
11 Blenheim Court, 316 Woodstock Road, Oxford OX2 7NS, England
www.johnbeaufoy.com

10 9 8 7 6 5 4 3 2 1

ISBN 978-1-906780-20-3 (hardback)
ISBN 978-1-906780-58-6 (paperback)

Printed and bound in Malaysia by Times Offset (M) Sdn.Bhd.

Previous page: Emerald green rice terraces at Hapao, near Banaue, in the
Cordillera Central mountains of northern Luzon.
Right: A dusk view of shoreside bungalows at the luxury Lagen Island
Resort, in Bacuit Bay, El Nido, Palawan.

Presenting
THE
PHILIPPINES

A Journey through the Archipelago

NIGEL HICKS

JOHN BEAUFOY PUBLISHING

Contents

Opposite above left: Early in the morning children cross the Palanan River on their way to school, close to the village of Palanan, on the northeast coast of Luzon.
Above: A stunning *Melithaea* species sea fan on a rock wall in Tubbataha Reef National Marine Park, Sulu Sea, Palawan.
Opposite: A jeepney in downtown Legaspi, with Mt Mayon, the Philippines' most active volcano towering above; southern Luzon.
Left: A coconut palm stands silhouetted against the dusk, along White Beach, Boracay.

Preface

"... captures the beauty, diversity and unity of the Philippines."

It is no easy task to capture the diversity of an entire country within the covers of a single publication, but with entertaining and informative text, linked to stunningly evocative photography, Nigel Hicks manages to do just that. Drawing on a broad knowledge of the Philippine environment, culture, people and daily life, Nigel has encapsulated in words and images much of the beauty and diversity of this tropical archipelago. In doing so, he brings together the apparently disparate subjects of the beaches that attract so many overseas visitors, Filipino livelihoods, religion and general way of life, and the stunning beauty of the country's natural environment and wildlife. The result is a superb portrait of the Philippine nation, a portrait that on the one hand shows the Philippines to be a hugely diverse island nation, and yet on the other illustrates its unity, a cluster of islands with a distinct, perhaps even unique identity.

It is hoped that over the coming few years *Presenting the Philippines* will be an immensely valuable book, of great interest to both overseas visitors and Filipinos alike. Visitors are likely to find it of value whether they are in search of a greater understanding of the country or simply would like a memento of an enjoyable visit. Filipinos – whether resident in the Philippines or overseas – will hopefully be drawn to it in order to have on their bookshelves a beautiful volume that in both words and pictures captures the beauty, diversity and unity of the Philippines.

Left: A *banca*, or outrigger boat, the ubiquitous Philippine ferry and fishing boat used throughout the islands, sits on its mooring in the shallow, crystal clear waters of Small La Laguna Beach in Puerto Galera.
Following page: Terraced rice fields at the village of Batad, near Banaue, in the Cordillera Central range of northern Luzon.

THE PHILIPPINES

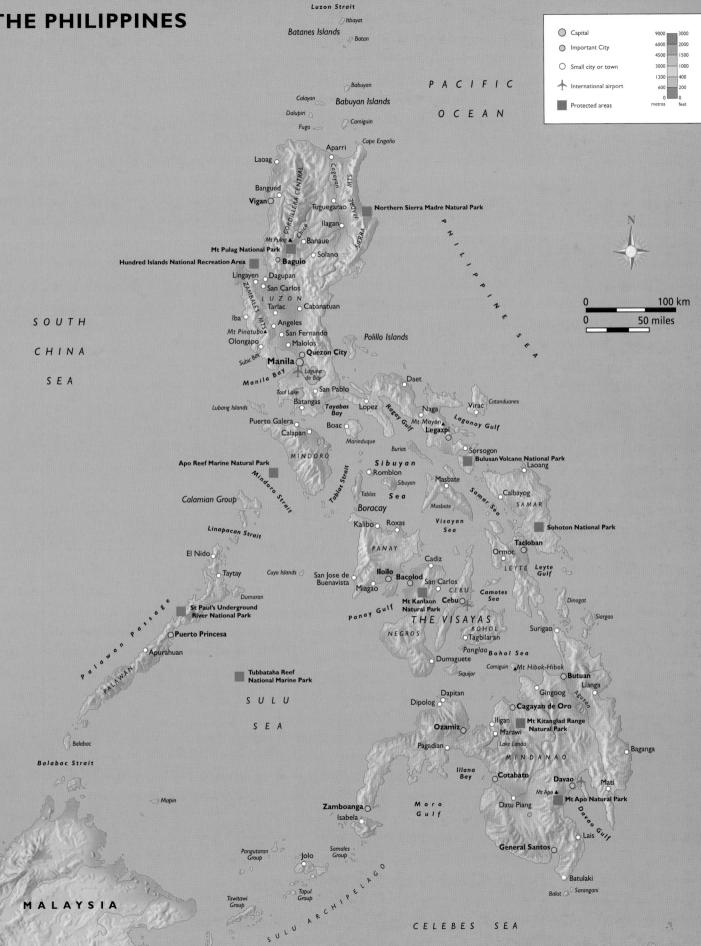

Luzon Strait
Itbayat
Batanes Islands
Batan

PACIFIC

OCEAN

Babuyan
Calayan
Babuyan Islands
Dalupiri
Fuga
Camiguin

Cape Engaño
Aparri
Laoag

Bangued
Vigan
Tuguegarao
Northern Sierra Madre Natural Park
Ilagan

Banaue
Mt Pulag ▲
Solano
Mt Pulag National Park
Baguio
Hundred Islands National Recreation Area

Lingayen
Dagupan
San Carlos
Tarlac
Cabanatuan
Iba
Angeles
Mt Pinatubo ▲
San Fernando
Olongapo
Malolos
Subic Bay
Quezon City
Manila
Manila Bay
Laguna de Bay
Daet
Taal Lake
San Pablo
Lubang Islands
Batangas
Tayabas Bay
Lopez
Naga
Virac
Catanduanes

Puerto Galera
Boac
Mt Mayon ▲
Lagonoy Gulf
Calapan
Legazpi

Marinduque

MINDORO
Sorsogon
Apo Reef Marine Natural Park
Burias
Bulusan Volcano National Park
Laoang

Calamian Group
Romblon
Masbate
Calbayog
SAMAR
Sibuyan
Samar Sea
Tablas
Masbate

Linapacan Strait
Boracay
Visayan Sea
Kalibo
Roxas
Sohoton National Park
El Nido
Cuyo Islands
Cadiz
Ormoc
Tacloban
Taytay
San Jose de Buenavista
Iloilo
San Carlos
LEYTE
Leyte Gulf
Dumaran
Miagao
Bacolod
CEBU
Camotes Sea
St Paul's Underground River National Park
Mt Kanlaon Natural Park
Cebu
Dinagat
Puerto Princesa
THE VISAYAS
BOHOL
Apurahuan
NEGROS
Tagbilaran
Surigao
Siargao
Panglao
Bohol Sea
Tubbataha Reef National Marine Park
Dumaguete
Camiguin
Siquijor
Mt Hibok-Hibok ▲
Butuan
Lianga
PALAWAN
SULU
Dapitan
Gingoog
Cagayan de Oro
Dipolog
Balabac
Ozamiz
Iligan
Mt Kitanglad Range Natural Park
Balabac Strait
Marawi
SEA
Pagadian
Lake Lanao
Baganga
MINDANAO
Mapin
Cotabato
Davao
Mt Apo ▲
Mati
Mt Apo Natural Park
Illana Bay
Datu Piang
Zamboanga
Isabela
Moro Gulf
Davao Gulf
General Santos
Lais
Pangutaran Group
Samales Group
Jolo
Batulaki
Tapul Group
Balut
Sarangani
Tawitawi Group
SULU ARCHIPELAGO

CELEBES SEA

MALAYSIA

SOUTH

CHINA

SEA

Polillo Islands

Ragay Gulf

Panay Gulf

Tablas Strait

Mindoro Strait

PANAY

PHILIPPINE SEA

CAGAYAN MTS
SIERRA MADRE
CORDILLERA CENTRAL
Chico
LUZON
ZAMBALES MTS
Aguan
Agusan

N

Legend	
○	Capital
○	Important City
○	Small city or town
✈	International airport
■	Protected areas

metres	feet
9000	3000
6000	2000
4500	1500
3000	1000
1200	400
600	200
0	0

0 ___ 100 km
0 ___ 50 miles

Introduction

Every one of the Philippines' main islands or island groupings has a unique feel: the landscape, the natural environment…the people…

Even the briefest glance at any map of the Philippines will reveal its principal defining feature: it can be described as a huge fractured mass of islands, the mother of all archipelagos, or a swathe of islands sitting on the western edge of the Pacific Ocean, stretching across much of the tropical belt north of the Equator, from close to Indonesia in the south and almost as far as China in the north.

It's a physical feature that immediately suggests another of its most important characteristics: diversity. Every one of the Philippines' main islands or island groupings has a unique feel: the landscape, the natural environment, the wildlife, the people and the economy are all rather different from its neighbours across the water. The result is a country that is profoundly different in its far north to the country in the far south, especially so in terms of the peoples that inhabit the landscape. And yet, despite the island sprawl and the great diversity across them, there is a unity throughout that makes them all distinctly Filipino.

What that distinct Filipino essence is, I struggle to put into words. Is it the colourful chaos of its towns and cities (hardly unique to the Philippines) or the brilliant smile that seems ready to erupt from any face at the slightest 'provocation'? Is it the friendly chatter, invariably in a mix of languages that forms a constant backdrop to urban and country life, the ready helpfulness extended to any stranger, or the generally relaxed and unhurried approach to the stresses and strains of life? Perhaps it's the heat and humidity, suffused with the smells of cooking and tropical fruit that hang in the air just about everywhere. Or maybe it's the intense, dark, almost brooding green of the tropical vegetation, whether farmland or forest, set against the blinding white coral sands of the beaches and the aquamarine blue of the encircling tropical seas. Actually the Philippines is all of these, and undoubtedly many more that combine to make a complex and intriguing country.

People and culture

For me, one of the most quintessentially unique Philippine features is its ability to absorb almost any kind of outside influence without fear or prejudice, mix it up, add a dash of the Philippines, and push it back out again as something quite distinct. Perhaps it's something that comes naturally to the Filipinos, or maybe it's a survival skill honed from hundreds of years of Spanish and then American colonial rule, but it really works, creating today's Philippines as a real cultural pot-pourri – some might say a mish-mash – of global influences. The result is a country in which, for example, Spanish surnames (and indeed Christian names too) are very common even though no one speaks Spanish any more, while English is the widely used language of choice for government and business.

The import that has had the greatest impact, however, is religion, essentially Catholic Christianity over much of the country, and Islam in the far south. One of only two Christian countries in Southeast Asia (the other being East Timor), Catholicism arrived with and was enforced by the islands' Spanish rulers. Today, about 90 per cent of Filipinos are Catholics, mostly quite devout in a way that genuinely influences daily life, while many of the churches they use are cultural monuments dating from the Spanish era.

Islam arrived from about the 13th century onwards, imported by Arab traders and missionaries who arrived mainly from what is now Indonesia, introducing the religion mostly to the far south of

Opposite above left: A fishing family work to pull fish out of a net, in the Siargao Islands, Mindanao.
Opposite above centre: A mangrove tree growing on sand flats, Olango Island, Cebu.
Opposite above right: A *bulul* effigy carved into a fence post as an agricultural protective deity, on the slopes of Mt Pulag, northern Luzon.
Opposite: The remarkable Chocolate Hills in central Bohol, one of the Philippines' iconic views, and so named for their brown colour at the end of the dry season.

the Philippines. Today, about 5 per cent of Filipinos are Moslem, and the religion is mainly practised in south-western Mindanao and the scattered Sulu islands that stretch down towards Indonesia.

The remaining 5 per cent of the Philippine population consists mostly of a plethora of small cultural or ethnic minorities, mostly practising animist religions, and often living in remote areas. Arguably most famous among these are the Aeta and Ifugao peoples, the former scattered mainly across Luzon and believed to be the country's aboriginal inhabitants. The Ifugao, on the other hand, live only in the steep mountain valleys of northern Luzon. Their ancestors built mighty rice terraces that to this day cover the mountainsides around the town of Banaue, today a UNESCO World Heritage Site and a major visitor attraction.

Above: Rice terraces on the edge of the village of Banaue, in the Cordillera Central mountains of northern Luzon.
Opposite: The Philippines has some of East Asia's most spectacular beaches. This one on Pandan Island, off the west coast of Mindoro, is quite remote, but its beauty amply rewards the effort of getting there!

Beaches and relaxation

For the visitor, undoubtedly the main attractions are the country's stunning beaches, concentrated mainly in the central region, the Visayas. Here you'll find a great mass of small islands, many almost completely ringed by white coral sand, the quintessential tropical island paradises and truly the stuff of many a Robinson Crusoe-inspired dream.

Head and shoulders above the competition, the Philippines' most popular attraction is undoubtedly Boracay, a tiny island in the western part of the Visayas, just off the northern tip of Panay, one of the region's main landmasses. Just a few kilometres long and less than two wide, Boracay became famous in the 1980s for its stunning, but nevertheless rather unimaginatively named White Beach, which stretches along much of the island's west coast, and is arguably one of Southeast Asia's most beautiful beaches.

There are plenty of other great beach locations, of course, including several – most notably Alona Beach – along the south coast of Panglao Island, part of Bohol in the Visayas' southeast. The best known beach area outside the Visayas is probably Puerto Galera, a remote but easily accessible beach-studded peninsula at the northern tip of Mindoro. Palawan is home to El Nido, a small town that sits deep inside Bacuit Bay, sheltered by a string of limestone islands around which are scattered some stunning beaches and equally stunning resorts.

There are of course, many other beaches gradually becoming more popular and others still waiting to be truly discovered. One such place is the spectacular but almost deserted beach at Sabang on Palawan, which to this day remains lightly used, despite being the entry point for the nearby and widely known St Paul's Underground River National Park.

Coral reefs and diving

Apart from lots of sand, one thing that almost all the beaches have in common is that they are great bases for diving trips to nearby coral reefs. Although many of the Philippines' reefs have been badly damaged by dynamite and cyanide fishing, quite a number have received at least partial protection from such things and remain in good condition. As a result, the Philippines offers some of the most spectacular scuba diving in the world, with sites – many very close to the beaches – that offer everything from shallow and stunningly beautiful coral gardens, to deep oceanic rifts populated by sharks and shoals of pelagic fish.

Not surprisingly, scuba diving is the number one sport for visitors not content to lie around on the beach, and with so many diving operators scattered around the country it's very easy to learn the skills and obtain the necessary certification.

Mountains and forests to explore

In recent years, tourism has begun to look inland, towards the country's volcanoes and mountain ranges. Largely overlooked as a visitor attraction until quite recently, hiking to the summits of the Philippines' countless volcanoes (the highest of which is nearly 3000 metres), is becoming increasingly popular. It has to be said that with facilities very limited on most mountains, and with trails steep, slippery and for the most part unmaintained, hiking here is usually not for the faint-hearted. However, for those with the energy and the gung-ho spirit, hiking in the Philippines' mountains and forests represents a real taste of a wilderness challenge.

The most famous of the climbs is undoubtedly that up to the country's highest peak, Mt Apo, close to the city of Davao in the far south. Taking a minimum of two days, this is perhaps the most well-organized of the country's hiking routes, with hiking permits, guides and supplies readily available and the route reasonably clear.

Unique wildlife

Venturing into the mountain ranges on foot inevitably brings the visitor into very intimate contact with the Philippines' forests and volcanoes, but that doesn't usually mean a clear and intimate view of the wildlife. While scuba divers will quite definitely get to see a huge range of marine wildlife, in the forests and mountains most animals are shy and remain hidden. It is a shame, because most of the Philippines' land-based wildlife is quite unusual. The islands' isolation from both mainland Asia and from each other has generated bird, mammal, reptile and amphibian wildlife that is quite unique, with a huge proportion of Filipino species limited not just to this country but actually to a few – or even one – island within the archipelago. Once again, we are back to the Philippines' diversity.

King among this uniqueness is the huge Philippine Eagle, now confined to a few of the country's mountainous forest regions. Hikers on Mt Apo and Mt Kitanglad might just get a glimpse if they're really lucky. Also of great importance is the Tamaraw, a dwarf buffalo restricted to a few forest locations on Mindoro, and the Philippine Tarsier, a tiny primate unique to Mindanao and the eastern Visayan islands, though related to a similar tarsier on Borneo. Completely unheard of outside the Philippines are the Bleeding-heart pigeons, so named for the splash of red on their chests. There are five species of this pigeon, all unique to different Philippine island groupings, an evolution clearly illustrating the islands' geographic isolation from one another.

All this just serves to highlight the beauty, diversity and uniqueness of the Philippines. Much of what has been introduced here will be described in greater detail in the following chapters, so read on, enjoy and then head off and discover it all for yourself!

This page: A dusk view across Taal Lake towards Taal Island and the Taal volcano, seen from the village of Talisay, on the edge of the Taal caldera, in southern Luzon (top). The Ruddy Kingfisher, *Halcyon coromanda*, is a lovely bird of mangroves and forest streams in Palawan and the Sulu archipelago. (above).

Opposite page: A lovely *Dendronephthya* species soft tree coral, growing on the reef wall around Balicasag Island, Bohol (above). A *banca* moored in the shallows alongside Yapak Beach, on Boracay (below).

Chapter One
The Landscape

The official tally for the Philippine archipelago is 7107 islands: ranging from tiny flat sandbars and craggy treeless rocks to the mountainous, verdant main landmasses that the 90-plus million Filipinos call home. It all adds up to 300,000 km^2 of land (186,000 sq miles) – roughly 25 per cent bigger than Great Britain and about the same size as the US state of Arizona – all of it ringed by sparkling blue tropical seas. The country is separated from the main Asian landmass by deep oceanic trenches that have ensured the Philippines' isolation ever since these islands rose up from the sea bed millions of years ago. It all makes for a fascinating and wonderfully varied archipelago, not dissimilar from other Pacific Ocean islands or Southeast Asian countries, and yet also quite distinct from all of them.

Opposite above left: Dense undergrowth and the trunk of a giant tree in lowland rainforest around El Nido, in northern Palawan.

Above: A coral reef teeming with life around Pescador Island, close to Moalboal, Cebu.

Opposite left: A classic tropical coastline, lined with forest and protected by an offshore fringing reef, seen on Danjugan Island, off the coast of Negros.

Left: Early morning light and mist in the mountains of the Cordillera Central range, in northern Luzon.

The Landscape

"One of the biggest volcanic eruptions the world experienced in the 20th century was that of the Philippines' Mt Pinatubo."

The Philippines lies on the western edge of the Pacific Ocean, separating the open ocean to the east from the more enclosed South China Sea to the west. The nearest non-Philippine landmass is the Malaysian and Indonesian island of Borneo to the southwest, less than 40 km (25 miles) from the nearest Philippine islands in the Sulu archipelago. To the north, the nearest country is Taiwan, which is almost 200 km (about 120 miles) from the nearest Philippine islands, the remote and windswept Batanes group. The Philippines has no land borders.

Place and form

Much of the country can be divided into just five island groups that make up the great majority of the total land area. The largest is Luzon, covering the northern half of the country and site of Manila, the national capital. Luzon can be divided into northern and southern main sections.

The northern section is a roughly oval-shaped mountainous region, consisting of several north-south running ranges. Luzon's southern section is a very long and narrow peninsula, known as Bicol, which extends for hundreds of kilometres to the southeast.

Mindanao is the country's second largest island, making up the southernmost main landmass. Like northern Luzon, it is very mountainous and the site of Mt Apo, the country's highest mountain (2954 m/ 9691 ft). A string of separatist insurrections (see Chapter 2), these days mostly restricted to the west and southwest of the island, have ensured that many parts of Mindanao remain wilder and less developed than many other parts of the country.

Separating Luzon and Mindanao are the Visayas, a fractured mass of islands, the most significant of which are Cebu, Negros, Bohol, Panay, Samar and Leyte. Many of the Visayan Islands are sheltered from the Pacific both by Luzon's Bicol peninsula and the easternmost part of the Visayas, namely Samar and Leyte. The more protected areas are home to some of the Philippines' most spectacular beaches, such as those on Panglao Island and Boracay, the latter arguably one of Southeast Asia's most magnificent beach resorts.

Nestling in close to the southwestern corner of Luzon is Mindoro, an extremely wild and mountainous island, still relatively thinly populated and much of it quite inaccessible.

Last, but not least, of the five island groups is Palawan, an incredibly long, pencil-thin island group that stretches in a northeast-to-southwest direction, reaching from some way off the southwestern side of Mindoro almost down as far as the northeast coast of Borneo. Much of Palawan is still wild and forested, though how long this will last is open to question, as its population is rising rapidly due to inward migration from the more crowded areas of the country.

Apart from these five major island groupings, there are a number of other minor island groups, most rather remote, such as the Batanes islands midway between Taiwan and the main Luzon landmass, and the Sulu islands stretching southwest from Mindanao down to within a few kilometres of the east coast of Borneo.

Above: The stunning White Beach on Boracay Island, the Philippines' number one attraction.
Opposite: The sweeping slopes and smouldering pinnacle of Mt Mayon, the Philippines' most active volcano.

The forces of earthquake and volcano

The archipelago does not form just the western edge of the Pacific Ocean, but also the western arc of the Pacific Ring of Fire, that huge earthquake-prone and volcano-riddled series of fault lines that sweep almost the whole way round the Pacific. That fact alone says much about the Philippines' origin. Very little of the country has ever been a part of the main Asian landmass, the great majority of it rising up from the sea bed as a result of tectonic forces, driven on by the combined power of earthquake and volcano.

The landscape is littered with volcanoes, mostly inactive (but not necessarily dead), though 22 are classed as active, some of which are constantly watched by the Philippine Institute of Volcanology and Seismology (or PHIVOLCS for short). These range from the tiny Taal volcano, situated on an island in a vast caldera lake, to the massive Mt Kanlaon, at 2465 m (8087 ft) the highest mountain in the Visayas. The most active of all the country's volcanoes is undoubtedly Mt Mayon, which is known to have erupted almost 50 times, most recently in 2007.

A mighty volcanic eruption

One of the biggest volcanic eruptions the world experienced in the 20th century was that of the Philippines' Mt Pinatubo. Situated in the Zambales mountain region of northern Luzon, about 90 km (56 miles) north of Manila, it had been apparently inactive for about 400 years, but suddenly sprang to life early in 1991. In June of that year Mt Pinatubo almost literally exploded, knocking 300 m [984 ft] off its height, swamping towns and thousands of square kilometres of land in ash, and shutting down two of the USA's biggest overseas military bases, Clark Air Force Base and Subic Bay naval port. The situation was not helped by the arrival of a typhoon just as the eruption was dying down, which washed millions of tonnes of lahar, or volcanic mud, down the mountain and out across the already devastated lowlands.

In all, about 700 people died, mostly from the lahar flows. Pinatubo has not erupted since, but both the mountain itself and the land for miles around still resemble a lunar landscape.

Lakes, rivers and waterfalls

Being so mountainous, the country is criss-crossed by a large number of fast-flowing but rather short rivers, hardly any of which are navigable for any great distance. The country's longest river is the Cagayan, which meanders its way through one of the few flat lowland areas, a valley that divides two of northern Luzon's three mountain ranges, the Cordillera Central to the west and the Sierra Madre to the east. The river travels northwards, fed by both mountain ranges before it reaches the sea close to Luzon's northernmost tip, at the town of Aparri.

Lakes are a common feature of the Philippine landscape, the largest of these Laguna de Bay, lying right on the southern fringes of the capital city, Manila. Laguna de Bay is so vast it can at times more closely resemble an inland sea than a lake; it is nevertheless quite shallow and in many places no more than a few metres deep. Being close to Manila, its shores are heavily populated, putting the lake under enormous pressure, both from over-fishing and pollution.

Most lakes are volcanic in origin, formed by the flooding of calderas. The biggest and most spectacular is Lake Taal, a short distance south of Laguna de Bay. Formed in a vast ancient caldera, the best view of the lake is from the caldera's rim, high above the water and at an altitude of 700 m (2296 ft) above sea level. This rim marks the remains of a once vast volcano that erupted and collapsed aeons ago, leaving this enormous caldera. The lake itself was once a bay connected to the sea, but lava from an eruption several hundred years ago filled in the mouth of the bay, creating today's lake, which is now wholly fresh water. As already mentioned, the volcano is still active, with the active crater located on an island in the lake.

With terrain steep and rainfall high, it is undoubtedly waterfalls that take pride of place as the most spectacular of the Philippines' inland water features. Untold numbers of downward-rushing mountain rivers tumble time and again over cliff edges to create stunningly beautiful vertical ribbons of water, often falling into clear pools surrounded by dense forest. Many are perfect spots for enacting Tarzanesque dreams!

There are so many waterfalls it is hard to know where to begin when trying to highlight a few. Some favourites among the many would include the near-vertical column of water that is Pulang Tubig Falls, in Northern Negros Forest Reserve, Magasawang Falls on the lower slopes of Mt Kanlaon, also on Negros, and Malabsay Falls, in Mt Isarog National Park, southern Luzon.

The plant and animal world

Not surprisingly, millions of years of isolation from any other major landmass has led the Philippines' land-based wildlife – both plant and animal – to develop along its own particular path. The result is a stunning array of wildlife that is quite unique to these islands, so much so that the Philippines is classed as one of the world's nine biodiversity hotspots. It's an accolade that makes conservation in the islands crucial to the world's biodiversity as a whole.

Although cataloguing wildlife in the Philippines is far from complete, a look at just a few of the numbers that are presently known illustrates why this is so. Of the roughly 560 bird species (the animal group that has received the most study) 44 per cent are known to be endemic, or unique to the Philippines; while for mammals the proportion is even higher – an amazing 64 per cent of approximately 180 species, with new species still being found fairly regularly. Work with reptiles and amphibians is still ongoing, but the endemic percentage is eventually likely to be at least as high as that for mammals, and it is anyone's guess what will be found with the thousands of insect species still waiting to be examined. With 13,500 species of plants, it is believed that about 3200 may be endemic to the country, with species ranging from tiny mosses and grasses right up to some of the giant rainforest trees. An example of the latter is the almaciga, or Philippine mahogany, one of the largest trees in the Philippine rainforest.

Overwhelmingly, tropical rainforest is the Philippines' principal natural environment, and inevitably, the great majority of the Philippines' land-based wildlife has evolved to live in this environment. These include several species of deer and warty pig, as well as a steadily growing list of cloud-rat species, plus a host of different types of bat. These range from the tiny bamboo bat which is as small as a thumbnail and hides in cracks in bamboo, to a number of species of giant fruit bat that congregate in large, mixed flocks hanging from the branches of some of the forests' tallest trees. Monkeys are remarkable for being almost completely absent, their only representative being the Long-tailed, or Crab-eating macaque, which can be found in a number of places in the country, most especially Palawan. Another primate is the Philippine Tarsier, a tiny and rather cute nocturnal animal that is restricted to Mindanao and some parts of the eastern Visayas, and which is related to a similar species in Borneo.

Being forest dwellers, these animals – with the exception of some of the fruit bats – are rather shy and make a point of remaining hidden most of the time. It is for this reason that the Philippines' birds have received the most attention, though even these can be hard to spot in the forest. However, in places where hunting has not been a problem and there are reasonably accessible forest clearings, a great range of birds can be watched.

Top: The Palawan Peacock Pheasant, *Polyplectron emphanum*, is endemic, or unique, to Palawan.
Above: Giant trees still dominate the lush lowland rainforest found in Subic Bay Forest Reserve, some of Luzon's best surviving rainforest.
Opposite: Malabsay Falls, surrounded by verdant rainforest on the lower slopes of Mt Isarog, southern Luzon.

King among the birds is the endemic Philippine Eagle. Standing over 1.5 m tall (5 ft), it is the world's second largest eagle (after the Harpy Eagle of South America). Like the Harpy, it is a forest species, an unusual habitat for eagles, but the Philippine Eagle is often spotted flying through the trees rather than high above the canopy. Dependent on healthy rainforest, its range has shrunk over the past 50 years (see box story), but it is still found across mountainous Mindanao, as well as being present on the islands of Samar and Leyte and in northeast Luzon.

Perhaps the most common birds are pigeons, not the dull grey urban variety, but wonderfully varied and colourful forest species that include various shades of pink, green, yellow, brown and red. Other easily recognized species include hornbills, of which there are at least seven species in the Philippines, some of which are now quite rare. They are easily recognized by their huge bills and the enormous helmet-like casque that sits above the bill. Perhaps the most commonly seen of these are the Palawan Hornbill, not surprisingly restricted to Palawan, and the Rufous Hornbill, most commonly seen in northern Luzon.

One of the most remarkable features of the Philippines' biodiversity is just how much variation there is around the country. Philippine species evolved not just in isolation from the main Asian landmass but also from each other on neighbouring islands. Biologists have been able to divide the country into five biogeographic regions based on island groupings and the presence of island-to-island linkages during the last ice age, about 10,000 years ago; when sea levels were 120 m (400 ft) lower than today. These essentially follow the same geographical divisions described earlier, with the exception that the islands of the eastern Visayas (principally Bohol, Samar and Leyte) belong to the Mindanao biogeographic division. As a result, many Philippine endemic species may be limited to islands within just one of the country's biogeographic regions.

The outside influences that did reach the Philippines are often limited to just the nearest of the country's biogeographic regions. For example, some plants commonly found in southern China and Taiwan also appear in parts of Luzon, but nowhere else in the Philippines. Similarly, mammals commonly found in Borneo also have close relatives in the Mindanao region, though no other part of the Philippines; these include the Flying Lemur and the already mentioned Philippine Tarsier.

Moreover, the Philippines sits on one of the world's major biogeographic divisions, the Wallace Line, named after Alfred Wallace, a 19th century biologist and contemporary of Charles Darwin, who identified this division. Running roughly north-south, the line passes between Palawan and the rest of the Philippines, and identifies a tendency for species of Asian origin to exist to the

Top: The Philippine White-winged Flying Fox, *Pteropus leucopterus*, is a large fruit bat endemic to the Philippines, dependent on healthy rainforest to survive.
Above: The tiny Philippine Tarsier, *Tarsius syrichta*, is endemic to Mindanao and the eastern Visayas, but related to a similar tarsier found in Borneo.

west, and a tendency for species originating from Australasia to exist to the east. The Philippines (with the exception of Palawan) sits east of the line in the northern part of a transition zone called Wallacea, in which a steady shift from Asian to Australasian species occurs as one moves east and south. The fact that neither eucalyptus trees nor marsupial mammals made it to the Philippines does not upset the apple cart on this one, since both almost managed the leap, reaching as far as Indonesian islands just a short distance to the south.

The coast and its reefs

With so many islands, not surprisingly the Philippines has a truly extensive coastline. The great majority is quite gentle and unremarkable, many areas forming coastal plains that end in a low rocky 'table' that drops just a few metres straight into the sea, the remains of ancient coral reefs raised above sea level.

Quiet coves may seem to gradually merge with the sea, terra firma screened from the water by sometimes extensive bands of mangrove forest, whose roots are able to tolerate daily saltwater flooding. These often narrow forest bands not only protect the land behind from the sea's wave action, but also trap sediment to help build up more land, and moreover offer a protected home to a vast array of fish and crustacean larvae, helping to support sea-life and hence the fisheries.

Of greatest interest to the visitor are the dazzling white sandy beaches, often backed by manmade coconut groves to create the quintessential tropical paradise. This sand is generally finely ground-up coral – hence its dazzling bright whiteness – all that remains in the final stage of many a coral reef's lifecycle.

It is the coral reefs that justifiably make the Philippine coast famous. Shielding large stretches of shoreline from potentially damaging surf, the reefs are an essential partner to the coastline. Coral is of course a tiny but nevertheless living, breathing animal existing in vast colonies that together build up a huge non-living limestone framework on which they spend their immobile lives. It is this limestone structure that we think of as the solid, rocky reef and which eventually forms the sand of those lovely beaches. But it is the millions of tiny coral organisms that give the reefs their huge variety of colours and forms.

It is believed that the Philippines' reefs consist of about 500 species of coral, and that along with Indonesia and Malaysia form the epicentre of global coral biodiversity and distribution. What is more, the complex reef structure, with its vast numbers of nooks and crannies provides an ideal home for a huge range of mobile sea-life from fish larvae, through small sea slugs and snails, crabs and lobsters and an enormous diversity of small fish that live only on reefs, to large predatory species such as barracuda, tuna, dolphins and sharks. Altogether, the coral reef environment is a mind-boggling display of nature's beauty and diversity.

Top right: A healthy natural environment, mangroves lining a coastal creek, giving way to dense rainforest, seen on Sibuyan Island in the Visayas.

Centre right: Dense mangroves, complete with a tangle of aerial roots, in a sheltered cove on Danjugan Island, Negros.

Below right: An assortment of corals on a healthy reef off the coast of Puerto Galera, Mindoro.

The natural environment in crisis

What has been described above is the type of natural world that can be found in the Philippines, and which would be seen right across the country if its natural environment were in good health. Sadly, this is not the case, and today much of that natural environment is fragmented and struggling to survive against huge pressures.

It is estimated that at the start of the 20th century over 90 per cent of the country was forested, most of it pristine primary forest that had never been touched by mankind. Today, only about 6 per cent of that primary forest remains, with a further 15 per cent or thereabouts, covered with secondary forest, that is forest that has at least partially regrown and/or recovered from damage. The decline of the forests began with the American colonial era (1899-1946), when systematic logging started, and went into overdrive following independence. The damage caused by logging has been compounded by the farming methods of a poor and rapidly growing rural population, who – constantly desperate for new farmland just to survive – have followed the logging roads ever deeper into the forests. Commercial logging continues today, particularly in eastern Mindanao, despite protests and some sporadic bans.

As a result, many forest areas are badly fragmented, often surviving as islands of nature isolated from one another in a sea of human development. Not surprisingly, lowland rainforest has been most badly hit, due to its relatively easy access and presence of the biggest trees. In Luzon, the only truly extensive lowland rainforest that remains today lies along the very remote northeast coast, protected from incursion by the Sierra Madre Mountains. A smaller area survives around Subic Bay, until 1992 the USA's largest overseas naval base, and a very small patch also survives at the base of Mt Makiling, protected inside the Los Banos campus of the University of the Philippines. Other areas of lowland rainforest survive on the Visayan Islands of Samar, Leyte, Panay and Negros, and in the mountainous and less settled parts of Mindanao. How long Palawan's extensive stands of lowland rainforest can survive the rapid immigration presently occurring from the more populous parts of the Philippines remains to be seen.

Forests on the higher mountain slopes have faired rather better, largely due to their remoteness, altitude and steep volcanic terrain – places that are generally too steep, too cold and too rainy to farm easily, and often too close to an active volcano to be safe. However, even these are coming under pressure. On Mt Dulang-Dulang, part of Mindanao's Kitanglad range and the country's second highest mountain, montane rainforest is being cleared by peasant farmers forced ever higher up the mountain slopes by population pressure and vast pineapple plantations on better land lower down. In the Cordillera Central of northern Luzon, montane rainforest is

Top: A view of rural Cebu, showing fragmented rainforest, broken up by steadily expanding farmland.
Above: The wreckage of a coral reef destroyed by dynamite fishing, seen on Tubbataha Reef, in the Sulu Sea.

naturally replaced by pine forests, the only pines native to the Philippines, but in many areas many of these pines have been lost to farming.

With so much of the country's wildlife adapted to the rainforest, the dramatic loss of this environment is serious news, especially for those species endemic to limited areas. As a result, almost all of the country's endemic species are endangered, and some may already be extinct. Of the Bleeding-heart Pigeons, only the Luzon and Mindanao species seem to be holding on reasonably well, while

Saving the Philippine Eagle

Fragmentation of the Philippine rainforest has greatly reduced the amount of habitat available to this huge eagle, and today it survives only in the remote forests of the Sierra Madre mountain range of northeastern Luzon, on the Visayan islands of Samar and Leyte, and in the forests of Mindanao. Estimates of its wild population are no more than guesses, and vary from 180-500 birds scattered across these isolated pockets, making the eagle in imminent danger of extinction. This, together with declining wildlife numbers remaining for the birds to hunt, has brought the eagles into ever greater conflict with human populations, as they start to help themselves to domestic livestock.

Mindanao seems to be a Philippine Eagle stronghold, and it is here that efforts to protect it have been concentrated. Since the late 1980s the Philippine Eagle Foundation (PEF), based just outside the city of Davao, has been the main focus of conservation efforts. Since foundation it has greatly extended the amount known about the eagle's distribution and lifestyle, hugely improved its standing both nationally and among the affected Mindanao rural populations, and made some inroads into working out how to breed the eagles in captivity.

Such work has led to the creation of two new protected areas, one on Mindanao, the other on Samar, specifically to protect known Philippine

Eagle populations. However, despite this and the fact that many eagles live in already existing protected areas, such as Mt Apo and Northern Sierra Madre Natural Parks, it is likely that most continue to live on unprotected lands, where they are susceptible to attack by hunters and aggrieved farmers.

The aim of captive breeding is to enable birds to breed in safety and then release them back into the wild in suitable sites not occupied by the declining wild population. Success has been mixed, but since 1992 the PEF has managed to breed 18 birds. In 2004, one was released as an experiment into a well monitored area of forest on the slopes of Mt Apo Natural Park. All went well initially, but after six months it was killed after landing on live electricity wires. In 2008 a second was released, but this was illegally shot and eaten by a farmer, illustrating the severe threat the bird faces.

Work continues, and for visitors a trip to PEF's site near Davao, where 36 eagles live in large aviaries, represents virtually the only opportunity to get to see these magnificent birds.

Above: The nation's conservation emblem, the Philippine Eagle, *Pithecophaga jefferyi*, is on the brink of extinction.

the other three species seem to be on the brink. Hornbills, too, are struggling. While the Palawan and Rufous Hornbills seemingly appear to be common, others such as the Visayan Tarictic and Mindanao Writhed-billed Hornbills are hanging on by a thread. Iconic among all the birds, however, is the mighty Philippine Eagle, now the country's conservation emblem. Requiring huge areas of forest to successfully hunt, the Philippine Eagle has become seriously endangered as a result of deforestation, and is now found in only a few scattered areas. Attempts to save it from extinction are described in the above box.

Deforestation is impacting not just on the wildlife, but has started to directly affect human populations. Loss of tree cover causes soil erosion during the rainy seasons, leading to landslides, siltation of rivers and floods. In 1991, for example, during heavy typhoon rains a devastating flood hit the city of Ormoc, on the island of Leyte, killing 2000-6000 people and causing widespread destruction. The blame was laid squarely at the feet of illegal loggers operating in the hills nearby, but actually the root cause lay in long-term government policies that had seen tree cover on Ormoc's watershed reduced to just 10 per cent. Similar devastating floods and landslides hit the eastern Visayas in 2006, when the region was struck by three typhoons in quick succession, resulting in the deaths of an estimated 2000 people.

The coasts have suffered just as badly, with large areas of mangroves cut down to provide firewood and/or to make way for prawn farms. Most coral reefs have also been damaged or actually destroyed by a combination of dynamite and cyanide fishing, and siltation due to run-off from nearby deforested hills. It has been estimated that as a result only 5 per cent of the country's reefs remain undamaged.

Another threat to the reefs is increasingly frequent coral bleaching, caused by higher than normal ocean temperatures. Though corals can survive if this happens only occasionally, it is thought that frequent bleaching causes death. Hardly the fault of the Philippines, rising sea temperatures is a direct part of global warming, fuelled by the world's industrialised nations.

Conservation efforts

If all this sounds depressing, be assured that all is not completely lost, not yet anyway. Dynamite and cyanide fishing appear to be less common than they once were, and as a result many reefs are showing signs of recovery. A number of reefs close to popular beaches were declared marine reserves up to 20 years ago, and these have fared quite well, local communities recognizing a clear financial advantage to protecting them. Thus, it's no coincidence that the popular beach resorts of Puerto Galera on Mindoro, Boracay off the coast of the Visayan island of Panay, and Moalboal on Cebu, for example, all have magnificent coral reefs within easy boating distances.

Even reefs well away from popular resorts have come in for some protection, usually in the form of local ad hoc initiatives. In the 1990s it became clear that many fishing communities were over-fishing themselves towards extinction, caught in a poverty trap by steadily destroying the very resource that could help them to survive. Gradually, a few communities were persuaded to set up their own marine reserves over significant reefs, declaring no-fishing zones and limiting catches using traditional methods.

Initially, nearby communities who had not signed up to the creation of any local reserve strongly resisted, suspecting that they were just being thrown off their traditional fishing grounds. However, when the protected reef areas started to recover, improving catches in the fishing zones, more and more communities grasped the concept. Now there are over 1000 small-scale, locally-run marine protected areas around the coast. One of the earliest and most famous was set up in 1996 at the village of Handumon, on the north coast of Bohol, following initiatives by Canadian biologist Amanda Vincent. This initiative protected both declining seahorse populations and the coastal communities that harvested them. Project Seahorse has been so successful that not only has it spread along the Bohol coast but its work has become international.

On a larger scale, an ambitious programme to protect and restore coral reefs around Southeast Asia's core coral reef region has been launched. Covering the Philippines, Malaysia, Indonesia, Papua New Guinea and the Solomon Islands, it is called the Coral Triangle Initiative and involves a host of governments and international conservation organizations.

On land, a network of national parks was established by the American colonial government, but following independence little

was done to manage and enforce conservation within their boundaries. Logging and farming encroachment continued, causing many parks to become seriously degraded. By the 1980s, a number of international conservation organizations, such as the World Wide Fund for Nature (WWF), Fauna and Flora International (FFI) and Conservation International (CI) were getting involved in Philippine conservation.

The UN declared the whole of Palawan a protected area, integrating it into their global network of Man and the Biosphere reserves, though it is not clear whether this made much difference to life on the ground. In the mid-1990s, the World Bank and the European Union, working separately but in parallel along with the Philippine government's Department of the Environment and Natural Resources (DENR), started to establish what they called a Priority Protected Areas System, consisting of 20 large areas which,

Top: Conservation workers show off a captively bred Philippine Serpent-Eagle, *Spilornis cheela*, at the Philippine Raptor Center, on the lower slopes of Mt Makiling, Los Banos.

Above and opposite: Forestry workers in Mt Isarog National Park, Luzon, prepare to transport tree seedlings from their nursery to areas where they will be planted out, as part of a programme of rainforest restoration.

if protected, would ensure the survival of most of the Philippines' habitats and many of its endemic species. The programme reinvigorated Philippine conservation, but in 2002, when it reached the end of its first phase both the World Bank and EU pulled out. Today, the DENR continues to manage these sites with help from a network of Non-government organizations (NGOs), both Filipino and international, including CI and the WWF. There have been some notable successes, managing to bring into protection a huge area of rainforest in the Sierra Madre mountains of northern Luzon, more or less doubling the already vast area protected under the priority protected areas programme.

Climate

The Philippines is a wholly tropical country and is hot and humid all year round, with temperatures generally around 28–35°C and humidity at 80-98 per cent. It also has a very high rainfall, ranging from about 2000 mm (80 in) annually in Manila, to around 4000 mm (160 in) in many mountain regions, and up to a staggering 10,000 mm (400 in) in the wettest mountain areas.

The weather, and most especially rainfall pattern, is controlled by two seasonal monsoons, or prevailing wind directions: the southwest monsoon, which blows from April or May to October or November, and the northeast monsoon, which lasts the rest of the year. Both winds travel across large tracts of open water before reaching the Philippines, allowing them plenty of time to suck up water – and hence potential rainfall – before hitting the islands. As a result, the annual rainfall pattern varies hugely across the country depending upon local exposure to the two monsoons. Those areas exposed to the southwest monsoon will receive heavy rain from June to October or November, while those facing the northeast will be wettest from November through to about March. Those unlucky areas exposed to both monsoons will be wet throughout much of the year. The only period when the whole country is likely to be reasonably dry is April-May, when there is something of a lull. The Filipinos call this brief dry window their summer, and it is by far the best time to go mountain hiking.

In addition to the monsoon seasons, from April to November there is the constant threat of typhoons, intense tropical storms packing very high wind speeds and torrential rain. Although this is the southwest monsoon period, the typhoons develop out in the Pacific and track west or northwest towards Asia. Unfortunately, most make a beeline for the Philippines, slamming mainly into Luzon and regularly causing a vast amount of damage. Fortunately the southern half of the country, essentially Mindanao and parts of the Visayas, lie south of the typhoon belt, and though their east coast is often pounded by large waves from typhoons to the north, the south rarely gets hit by the storms themselves.

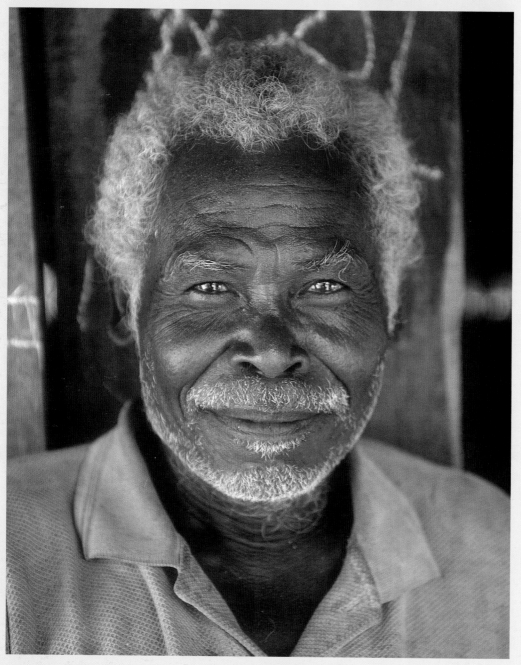

Chapter Two

The People

With a population of over 90 million, the Philippines can feel rather crowded, not just in the main cities but in many of the country areas too. It is indeed one of the most populated countries in Southeast Asia, only Indonesia – a far larger country – having more people. Not surprisingly, this crowding is at its most extreme in the cities, particularly the capital, Metro Manila, which with a population of almost 12 million – and growing fast – is by far the country's largest metropolis. Manila is a long way ahead of the next largest cities, Davao and Cebu, with about 1.4 million and 800,000 people respectively. Beyond these three big conurbations are a host of provincial towns and cities, the greatest concentration in the lowland areas just north and south of Manila. In fact, according to the Philippines' 2007 Census, over a third of the country's population lives in this central Luzon region.

Opposite above left: A Pinoy Filipino man shows off his young daughter; Puerto Galera, Mindoro.

Opposite above centre: A Negrito, or Aeta, woman with her young baby, at their forest camp along the coast of the far northeast of Luzon.

Above: Pinoy Filipinos stand to sing the national anthem during Independence Day celebrations, on 12th June, in Manila.

Opposite below left: A member of the Aeta, or Negrito, tribe, generally considered to be the Philippines' aboriginal people.

Left: A Santo Nino statue, an effigy of Jesus as a child, being carried by participants in the Ati-Atihan Festival, Kalibo.

The People

"The prominence of both Christianity and the English language are powerful defining aspects of today's Philippines…"

Across the countryside there are many small market towns and farming or fishing villages, concentrated mainly into either lowland areas or at least regions where the mountain slopes are not too steep for development. Population remains thin on the main mountain slopes, partly due to the problems of cultivation and heavy rainfall, but also – in the case of the many volcanic slopes – due to the danger of eruptions.

Two of the most immediately striking features of the Philippine people (or Filipinos, as they're usually known) are that, firstly, they constitute one of only two Christian countries in Southeast Asia, and secondly English is so widely spoken that it is one of the country's two official languages and very much the standard tongue of government and big business. These two facets are both tied up with the country's colonial past. In common with much

of the region, the Philippines spent a long time as a colony of a European power – in fact much longer than most – and this has had a profound impact. In the case of the Philippines, foreign control lasted almost 400 years, most of it under Spanish control, the final 50 years under the USA. Today, even the Filipinos joke that they spent 350 years in the convent and 50 in Hollywood!

The prominence of both Christianity and the English language are powerful defining aspects of today's Philippines, and give a strong indication of the extent to which the people are able to absorb outside influences and mould them into a part of the Philippine identity. However, there is a whole lot more beyond the effects of European colonialism, with origins stretching back well beyond the arrival of the Spanish. Unfortunately, with few pre-Hispanic records surviving, much has had to be pieced together using indirect evidence.

Filipino origins

The earliest remains of a human presence in the Philippines date back about 50,000 years to the Tabon Caves, located close to the west coast of Palawan. Finds at this site belong to an unknown ancestor, with no known links to any of today's Filipinos, not even the Aeta or Negrito, generally considered to be the country's aboriginal people,. Resembling the Aborigines of Australia, the Aeta have lived in the Philippines for at least 20,000 years and today they eke out a mainly nomadic existence in the remaining forests, and are in general, in steady retreat before the advance of the outside world.

The great majority of today's Filipinos are related to, but rather different from the Malays of Indonesia and Malaysia. It used to be thought that the Filipinos were descended from the Malays, but this is only partly true – in fact, if anything, the reverse is the case. What ethnologists now believe is that the great majority of today's Filipinos are descended from a group called the Austronesians, who migrated from their homeland in southern China or Taiwan about 5000 years ago, crossing the water directly from Taiwan into the north of the Philippines, and gradually spreading southwards. Once they reached the far south, they then split, one branch heading eastwards out into the Pacific to create today's Polynesians, the other turning west into Borneo, the other islands of today's Indonesia and finally into peninsular Southeast Asia, to form the ancestors of the Malays.

During historical times, this Austronesian Filipino population has been repeatedly modified by back-migration of Malays (mainly from Borneo) into various parts of the Philippines. One very well-documented of these Malay arrivals occurred on the Visayan island of Panay in the 13th century, when a group fleeing persecution in Borneo negotiated a land deal with the aboriginal Aeta people of Panay to allow them to settle there. To this day, this event is celebrated in two of the Philippines' most colourful and lively annual festivals, the Ati-atihan and Dinagyang festivals, both held in January in the Panay cities of Kalibo and Iloilo, respectively. Over the years, the descendents of that group spread out, and today make up much of the population of several Visayan islands and southern Luzon.

The Negrito people

Generally considered to be the Philippines' aboriginal people, and related to similar groups in Malaysia, Thailand and Papua New Guinea, the Negrito people have lived in the Philippines for at least 20,000 years. Though still surviving, they face huge challenges, not the least being the constantly expanding Filipino population and the steadily shrinking forests that they call home. Today, their numbers may be as low as about 15,000 and are steadily dwindling.

The typical Negrito is easily distinguished from the usual Filipino, being very dark-skinned and much shorter – rarely more than about 1.5 m (4.9 ft) tall – with high cheek bones and tightly curled hair. Calling themselves by a host of different names, most meaning simply 'man', such as Aeta, Agta, Ayta, Ita and Ati to name just the most common, many live a simple and fairly nomadic hunter-gatherer existence, mainly in northern Luzon's surviving forests., but also across many of the Philippines' other islands. Most also are small-scale farmers, and although often relatively shy, they frequently trade with their non-Negrito neighbours. Coastal Negritos with seafaring skills are usually called Dumagat, and these can be found along the very remote coast of northeast Luzon, such as around the village of Palanan, inside the Northern Sierra Madre Natural Park.

When it was part of the United States' Subic Bay Naval Base, Negrito tribesmen living in the rainforest surrounding the bay used to train American servicemen in jungle survival. Since the base's closure in 1992, they have done the same for visiting tourists, as well as running their own living 'museum' to Negrito life. This represents the best opportunity to get to meet the Negrito.

Other Negritos that have faired less well are those who used to call the forests that cloaked Mt Pinatubo their home. When the volcano erupted in 1991 (see Chapter 1), the forest and their home were destroyed, and many were lucky to escape with their lives. They were subsequently relocated to northern Mindanao, where they now live.

Above: Aeta children at play in the village of Pastolen, inside Subic Watershed Forest Reserve, Luzon.
Opposite: A colourful mass of dense traffic, consisting largely of jeepneys and motorized tricycles, clog up the centre of downtown Kalibo, Panay.

Ethnic and tribal minorities

Just how much Malay input has occurred over the years varies from one part of the country to another, giving rise at least to variation in regional characteristics, and in some cases to the establishment of some of the country's many tribal minorities. At one end of the spectrum are the people of the Sulu and Jolo islands, the archipelagos of small islands that stretch from the southwestern tip of Mindanao almost down as far as Borneo. Not surprisingly, these people, many belonging to the Tausug group, are actually largely Malay, and – being physically so much nearer the Islamic states of Indonesian Borneo than they are to the Christian cities of the northern Philippines – tend to have a much greater cultural and economic affinity with their Indonesian neighbours than they do with Manila.

At the other end of the scale, the remote Batanes islands, lying in the rough seas between the northern tip of Luzon and the southern tip of Taiwan, have had little immigration since the Austronesians arrived all those thousands of years ago. As a result, today's inhabitants, known as the Ivatans and numbering about 15,000, are thought to be almost pure Austronesian, with little, if any, Malay input. It has to be said that life here is hard, the islands cut off from outside contact and even supplies for long periods at a time due to the harsh weather. Electricity and cars arrived only in the 1990s. As knowledge of the outside world has grown, so the islands have struggled to maintain their population, and now some Ivatans have moved to set up new communities in Palawan.

Other cultural minorities with or without much Malay input over the years, have developed their own separate identities through prolonged isolation, not on remote islands but in isolated mountain valleys and ranges, particularly in the Sierra Madre and Cordillera Central ranges of northern Luzon. These minorities include such groups as the Ifugao, Bontoc and Kalinga, who all occupy different mountain regions of northern Luzon. The huge rice terraces that cover the mountain slopes around the town of Banaue, and which are now a UNESCO (United Nations Educational, Scientific, and Cultural Organization) World Heritage Site, were first built by Ifugao farmers 2000 years ago, and are still cultivated by their descendents today.

Almost the whole of Mindanao is rich in a wide diversity of tribal minorities, some of them Islamic. Non-Islamic groups include the Manobo, scattered across eastern Mindanao, including those in the floating raft villages of the vast Agusan Marsh, and also the T'boli in southern Mindanao. These and a number of Mindanao's other non-Islamic groups have in recent years given themselves the collective name 'Lumad', to distinguish themselves from the island's Moslem minorities.

Although the Tausug are perhaps the most well known of the Islamic minority groups, there are another nine, all concentrated in

Above: A Tagbanua man with his granddaughter, mending a fishing net on Coron Island, Palawan. The Tagbanua are shy rural people.

the western half of Mindanao, the Sulu archipelago and southern Palawan. Apart from the Tausug, the most important of these are the Maranao, Maguindanao and Yakan. The influence of Islam in the Philippines and its role in the life and culture of these groups will be described more fully below and also in Chapter 5.

Elsewhere, on Mindoro a rather shy group are the Mangyan, who still practise slash-and-burn farming on quite a large scale, and who have at times been quite hostile to what they consider to be outside interference by conservation organizations struggling to save what remains of the Philippines' rainforests. Another very shy group are the Tagbanua, just a few thousand strong and living mainly on the

small island of Coron, one of the Calamian Islands of northern Palawan. On Coron they live in a couple of remote, peaceful villages on the island's east coast, surrounded by jagged karst limestone pinnacles. The Tagbanua have traditionally protected their environment to ensure sustainability, a care that was formalized in the 1990s when the whole of Coron was declared a protected area by the Department of Environment and Natural Resources.

The Badjao, often known as Sea Gypsies, live in both Palawan and Sulu, as well as along coasts in a number of parts of Southeast Asia. Commonly seen living in boats or villages built on stilts out over water, the Badjao rarely come onto land, believing it to be a place of ghosts, used only as a graveyard for their dead.

One more group that has to be mentioned is the Chinese. Prominent across Southeast Asia, Chinese communities have been common in towns and cities throughout the region for about 1000 years, beginning with China's great heyday of international trading during the Tang and Song dynasties of the 7th to 14th centuries. Today's Chinese Filipinos consist of a mixture of descendents of immigrants who arrived in several waves over the past few hundred years, from the collapse of China's Ming dynasty in the 17th century, to the chaos of the Qing's decline and western imperial inroads into China in the 19th century. The most recent group consists of immigrants, and their offspring, who arrived following the Communist takeover of China in 1949.

As with their other communities all over Southeast Asia, the Chinese have retained their own ethnic and cultural identity down the years, while at the same time integrating into the Philippines. With a strong work ethic and entrepreneurial spirit, the Chinese have become major players in the Philippine economy, controlling large parts of its business and so wielding an influence far above their actual numbers.

This is just a sample of the Philippines ethnic or tribal minorities – there are many more. Yet, despite all this diversity, they make up only 10 per cent of the country's population, and half of these are all the various Moslem groups (only one of which is the Tausug). The remaining 90 per cent consists of what are considered to be the typical Christian Filipino, known affectionately by themselves as the 'Pinoy'.

Top left: A man of the Manobo cultural group, aboard a boat in the vast Agusan Marsh, central Mindanao.
Centre left: A typical home of the Ivatan people, on Sabtang, one of the Batanes Islands. Many Ivatan still lead a traditional life due to the isolation of their islands.
Below left: Chinese Filipino children putting on a martial arts display. Though a relatively small group, the Chinese are hugely influential due to their prominence in the Philippines' economy.

The Pinoy and the Philippines' languages

The Pinoy Filipinos occupy the great majority of the country, with the exception of a few parts of the far south, which are home to the country's Moslems. Although considered to be the 'typical' Filipino, they are not a single uniform group. Instead, they can be divided largely along linguistic lines, which themselves are defined mostly by regional groupings. There are believed to be over 80 languages and dialects in the Philippines, including many used only by the minorities, but the great majority of people speak as their native tongue just one of eight closely related languages: Tagalog, Cebuano, Hiligaynon (also called Ilongo), Waray-Waray, Ilocano, Pampangan, Pangasinan and Bicol.

Tagalog is the most common language, spoken in Manila and across much of northern Luzon. It has been used as the base for Pilipino, one of the country's two national languages (the other being English), created artificially from Tagalog and incorporating elements of the other major tongues. The next most common language is Cebuano, centred not surprisingly on the Visayan island of Cebu, but widely spoken across the Visayas. With so much immigration from other parts of the Philippines, in Palawan you're likely to hear every Filipino language there is, though the Visayan languages of Cebuano and Hiligaynon are particularly common. The latter is widely spoken across the Visayan island of Negros.

Although English is widely spoken in business and government, few people use it as their first language, preferring to speak whichever is their native Filipino tongue at home, and having to learn English at school. English is commonly used as the lingua franca for communication among people from the different Filipino language groups. Being derived from none of the Filipino tongues it is free from any political connotations, and the inference of northern Luzon's domination over the rest of the country, which Tagalog and Pilipino suffer from, and which is so resented by Cebuano speakers.

Visitors are often surprised that no one speaks Spanish. After all, the place abounds with Spanish names, both places and people, and a few Spanish phrases have been absorbed into the Philippine languages. Spanish was an official language even after the USA took over control of the country in 1899. However, in the early years of the 20th century it was replaced as the language of education by English, a move that inevitably saw the demise of Spanish within a generation, leaving just a wealth of Spanish names as its legacy.

Below: A Pinoy farmer paddling a simple canoe across Lake Balinsasayao, in the Southern Negros Forest Reserve, nr Dumaguete, Negros.

Religion

The greatest Spanish legacy is undoubtedly the country's Christianity, mostly Catholicism. Over 90 per cent of the population is Christian, with about 90 per cent of these Roman Catholic and the remainder belonging to an assortment of Protestant churches. There are two uniquely Philippine churches, the Iglesia ni Cristo, a Protestant church based on Unitarianism, and the Philippine Independent Church, a Catholic body that to this day remains independent of Rome. Both were set up at the beginning of the 20th century, the former centred around its founder, Felix Manalo, who styled himself the last messenger of God, and the latter in protest at the power of the Spanish priests. Today, Felix Manalo's church is headed by his son, has gone international and is now present in over 60 countries. With over three million members (the vast majority Filipinos), it is said to be larger than the Jehovah's Witnesses. In the Philippines, Iglesia ni Cristo is very visible right around the country to even the most casual observer, if only for its spectacular churches, built in concrete and painted white, with a uniform architecture of huge arches and soaring spires.

Catholicism has a very strong hold on the Philippines, the vast majority of the population very devout and fervent in their faith. Sunday attendance at mass is almost universal, coupled with visits to churches and personal prayer at other times. Belief in the power of statues and relics to grant favours and healing is widespread. The great majority of the Catholic churches date from the Spanish era, leaving a rich historical and architectural legacy (see the box on page 36), though sadly it has to be said that today most are looking distinctly care-worn and ragged, badly in need of some major restoration work.

A number of religious statues are greatly revered, none more so than the Santo Nino, a very old statue of Christ the child. This statue was originally presented to Ferdinand Magellan by the Spanish queen, to protect him as he set out from Spain on his epic 16th century voyage to find a westward route to the Spice Islands (now Indonesia). After reaching the Philippines in 1521, Magellan presented it to the wife of Rajah Humabon, the leading chief of Cebu, following his Christian baptism. Magellan was killed within days, leading one to wonder if perhaps he should have held onto the statue and its protective powers!

The statue was subsequently almost lost, but was rediscovered some years later by Magellan's successor Miguel Lopez de Legazpi. Today it is housed in the Basilica Minore in Cebu City, the centre of much worship and source of excellent business for the memento makers, who do a brisk trade in sale of replicas from stands and shops outside the Basilica.

Another famed and powerful statue is that of the Black Nazarene of Quiapo. Depicting Jesus as a black man, there are

Top: A stall selling religious mementos outside the Basilica Minore del Santo Nino, Cebu City.
Above: Vigan Cathedral, one of the Philippines' most elegant Spanish buildings; in Vigan, northern Luzon.

today numerous Black Nazarene statues in churches around the Philippines, but the original and most famous is at Quiapo Church in Manila. It was carved from wood in the 16th century in Mexico by an Aztec sculptor, and was shipped to the Philippines in 1606. It is believed that even the worst sins can be forgiven to anyone who prays before and touches the statue, ensuring chaotic scenes amid the huge crowd that gathers each time it is paraded through Quiapo's streets during the Black Nazarene Festival, held annually on 9th January.

The Spanish architectural heritage

Fragments of Spain's colonial rule of the Philippines lie scattered around the country, mainly in the form of a few fortifications and a great many churches. The best preserved example of domestic Spanish architecture, however, is the mestizo district of Vigan, a city in the far north of Luzon. Here an entire section of the city consists of streets lined wholly with Spanish era mansions, particularly along Calle Crisologo, where the only transport is horse-drawn carriages, or 'calesas'.

Well preserved fortifications include Fort San Pedro, in Cebu City, but the most famous is Intramuros, the old walled city of Manila, from which the Spanish controlled their colony. Unfortunately, although the immense walls are still intact, few of the original buildings inside survived intense fighting at the end of World War II, apart from the Church of San Agustin and its monastery, which today is a UNESCO World Heritage Site.

Above: A horse-drawn carriage, or *calesa*, on Calle Crisologo, the old Spanish district and World Heritage Site, in Vigan, northern Luzon.

Churches are the most widespread of Spain's architectural legacy, many built in a style that has become known as 'Earthquake Baroque', very elaborate and beautifully adorned but built with hugely thick fortress-like walls that could resist not only earthquakes but also anti-Spanish attacks. The oldest of these is the Church of the Immaculate Concepcion, at the village of Baclayon on the island of Bohol, while other fine examples include the church at the nearby village of Corella, and the cathedral in Vigan.

Four of the greatest churches are listed as UNESCO World Heritage Sites, including the already-mentioned Church of San Agustin, in Manila. The other three are another Church of San Agustin in Paoay, and Nuestra Señora in Santa Maria, both in the far north of Luzon, and also Santo Tomas in the village of Miagao, in southern Panay. They are all protected for the unique way local craftsmen have interpreted the European style. Miagao's church, completed in 1786, is a fine example, where the façade has been decorated with a carved coconut tree, depicting the tree of life, as well as numerous scenes and plants from Philippine life, a uniquely tropical theme imprinted on a typically European structure.

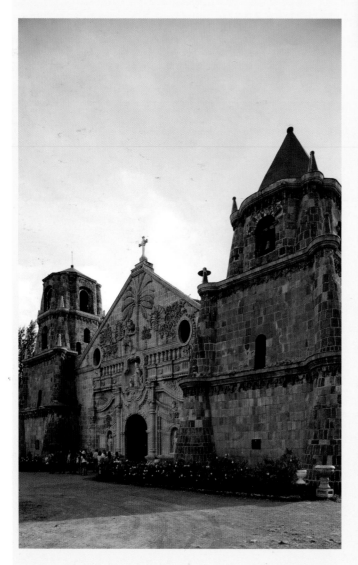

Left: The stunning facade of the Spanish-era Miagao Church, a UNESCO World Heritage Site, in the town of Miagao, near Iloilo, Panay.

As already mentioned, about 5 per cent of the Philippines' population is Sunni Moslem, concentrated in southern Mindanao as well as the Sulu archipelago of the far south. In this region the towers of Catholic and Protestant churches are replaced with the minarets of mosques. Arriving initially in the south of the country from the Indonesian islands after the 13th century, Islam has been firmly entrenched in this region since the 15th century. The first mosque was built on Simunul Island, in the Sulu islands, in the 14th century, and the first Islamic sultanate established in the Philippines in 1457. By the time the Spanish arrived in the 16th century, Islam had spread as far north as Manila, but it was quickly driven from these northern areas, retreating to its southern stronghold, where it remains today.

The Spanish called the Filipino Moslems 'Moros' (linked to the English word 'Moors', used to describe the north African Islamic invaders of Spain), a term that has stuck. To this day, the Filipino Moslems call themselves Moro, as a unifying term for the ten separate linguistic and cultural groups that make up the Philippines' Islamic population.

There have been numerous attempts down the years to weaken the Islamic hold over the south. Both the American colonial administration and the government of the newly independent Philippines in the 1950s encouraged Christians from the more crowded northern parts of the Philippines to settle in southern Mindanao. It was a process that greatly diluted the Moslem population and weakened their hold on land ownership. It also fuelled Moslem resentment, leading to a long-running battle for independence and the creation of a Moslem homeland, named Bangsamoro. This battle has been ongoing since the 1970s, and at times has been quite bloody, and although many Moslems have settled for autonomy within the Philippine nation, the armed struggle for full independence is still being waged by two organizations, the Moro Islamic Liberation Front (MILF) and Abu Sayyaf. This will be covered in greater detail in the next chapter.

Other religions include animism, Buddhism and Taoism, the last two practised mainly by the Filipino Chinese community. Ornate Chinese temples, largely painted red and filled with carvings of writhing dragons and statues of sages can be found in towns and cities throughout the country, though by far the most spectacular is the Taoist temple on the hillside above Cebu City.

Animism, the worship of spirits and deities in the natural world, including plants, animals and mountains, is practised by many of the country's tribal minorities, sometimes coupled with a thin veneer of Christianity. Visible expressions of animism can be seen in offerings, often of food, laid out beside fields planted with important crops, or wooden spirit effigies, often carved into fence posts outside homes or, once again, by fields of crops. Luzon's

Above: A woman presents a statue of Santo Niño, Jesus as a young child, during Dinagyang Festival, in Iloilo, Panay. Catholicism permeates almost all aspects of Philippine life, including its many festivals.

Cordillera Central is still a stronghold of animism, where the *bulul*, or rice gods are the most important manifestation of animism. Relics of past animist practices can still be seen, one of the most well known found around the lovely mountain village of Sagada in Luzon's Cordillera Central range, home of the Sagada cultural minority people, and where the deceased used to be laid to rest in coffins deposited in caves or hung from cliffs.

Chapter Three

A History of the Islands

Not so long ago, any history of the Philippines was likely to start in 1521, the year the islands were 'discovered' by Portuguese adventurer Ferdinand Magellan. His arrival paved the way for 400 years of colonial rule by western powers – mostly Spain – a period that saw the almost total destruction of evidence of much of what had come before the Europeans' arrival: the Philippines simply had not existed prior to 1521, or if it had, then anything its people had done simply did not matter.

Opposite above left: The entrance to Fort San Pedro, Cebu, the first permanent Spanish structure in the Philippines, built by Miguel Lopez de Legazpi in the mid-16th century.

Opposite above centre: The Magellan Monument on Mactan Island, Cebu, memorializes the death of Ferdinand Magellan near this site in 1521.

Above: The national flag of the Republic of the Philippines, symbolic of the anti-Spanish revolution at the end of the 19th century.

Opposite left: A statue of Lapu-Lapu on Mactan Island, Cebu, the Philippines' first national hero, renowned for killing Ferdinand Magellan in 1521.

Left: An old cannon on the ramparts of Taytay Fort, a Spanish fortification defending Taytay, their capital of Palawan.

A History of the Islands

"The Philippine islands developed extensive trade contacts with many other parts of Southeast Asia and China."

Fortunately, a lot of progress has been made in piecing together the life of the islands in the preceding centuries. It is known that the earliest remnants of human life date back as much as 750,000 years, found in the Cagayan Valley of northern Luzon. These remains, however, are believed to belong to *Homo erectus*, an evolutionary predecessor to modern humankind, *Homo sapiens*. The earliest signs of the latter come from the Tabon Caves, a cluster of over 200 limestone caves located at Lipuun Point on the west coast of Palawan. Several series of excavations here have yielded the oldest fossilized *Homo sapiens* bones to be found in Southeast Asia, which along with other artefacts show a continuous occupation of these caves from at least 50,000 to 9000 years ago. The caves are named after the Tabon Scrubfowl, a flightless bird that has also occupied the caves at various times, covering the cave floors with a thick layer of guano.

Philippine prehistory

Little is known about Tabon Man, as he has become known, except to say that he is not related to the Negritos, the earliest known settlers of the Philippines that survive today. The Negritos' origins, as well as when and how they arrived in the Philippines, remain a mystery, although – as described in Chapter Two – they are related to similar groups in Papua New Guinea and other parts of Southeast Asia. There is also evidence that they may be descended from the Australian Aborigines. The Negritos were almost certainly spread right across the Philippines by the time the Austronesians arrived from southern China and/or Taiwan 5000 years ago. The two groups are believed to have lived peaceably side by side; the Negritos' nomadic hunter-gatherer lifestyle and the Austronesians' settled agricultural society tending to complement each other rather than compete. However, the latter came to dominate, leading to the marginalisation and gradual decline of the Negritos which is in evidence today.

Later, came several waves of immigrants from Borneo and the Indonesian islands, many of which were refugees from persecution in their homelands. It is thought that the Mangyan people of Mindoro may be derived from one such migration. However, perhaps the most famous of these migrations was that of the 'Ten Datus', the 13th century arrival of ten chieftains and their people from Borneo. Landing on the island of Panay, they were able to negotiate a land deal with the local Negrito people that eventually saw them spread across much of the Visayas and southern Luzon, forming the basis of today's population.

Development and early international trade

Finds at the Tabon Caves and at other excavated sites around the country, show that the Philippine islands developed extensive trade contacts with many other parts of Southeast Asia and China. Before the arrival of Spanish colonial rule, no central authority arose to create a single Philippine nation. Instead, the archipelago consisted of a plethora of autonomous communities, or 'barangay', headed by local chieftains.

A number of coastal communities became important trading centres, particularly in the Sulu Islands, as well as the forerunners of today's Butuan, Cebu City and Manila. All three became closely tied in with at least one of the Southeast Asian kingdoms that rose and fell over the years, particularly the Vietnamese Champa kingdom (7th–19th centuries), the Sumatran Srivijaya kingdom (7th–13th centuries), the Javan Majapahit kingdom (13th–16th centuries) and Borneo's Kingdom of Brunei (14th–19th centuries). All of these, except Brunei, are often said to be 'Indianized' societies, in the sense that they had Hindu-Buddhist cultures, influences of which have also been found in early Philippine finds.

Written records from China's largest port, Quanzhou, on the southeast coast of Fujian province, show extensive trade with a number of Philippine ports during the Song and Yuan dynasties (960-1368 AD). Filipino traders were making regular visits to the Chinese port, while Chinese communities established themselves at several sites around the Philippine coast. Important Chinese centres developed at Butuan, then a major port on the northeast coast of Mindanao, as well as at Cebu and Manila, these two forming the early nuclei for today's major commercial conurbations.

Today's Manila metropolis arguably began life as the Kingdom of Tondo, a major trading centre on the north shore of and close to the mouth of the Pasig River, with extensive trade links with China. The earliest written reference to Tondo has been found on the Laguna Copperplate Inscription, a small sheet of copper found as recently as 1989 in mud close to Laguna de Bay, the lake just south of Manila. Dated to AD 900, the plate's inscription is written in the Kawi alphabet, at that time used in the Indonesian kingdom of Srivijaya. Kawi was similar to and ultimately derived from the alphabets of southern India, derivatives of which can still be seen today. Translated in the mid-1990s, its use of Kawi while at the same time referring to places in Luzon, provided evidence both of Tondo's importance and its links with the 'Indianized' Hindu-Buddhist kingdom of Srivijaya. Today, the plate is kept at Manila's National Museum.

Early in the 16th century Tondo was incorporated into the Kingdom of Brunei, subsequently spawning a second kingdom, Maynilad, on the southern side of the Pasig's estuary, which was also controlled by Brunei. Maynilad later became site of Intramuros, the fortified walled city that was the heart of Spanish Manila and the seat of the Philippines' colonial government. Tondo, on the other hand, has become one of the poorest parts of Manila, and with a population density of almost 70,000 people per square kilometre, one of the most crowded places on Earth.

Top: A sunset view across the marina to the modern tower blocks of the Ermita and Malate districts of Manila, part of the modern face of the capital.
Above: The Pasig River in the district of Binondo, close to where the earliest pre-Spanish settlements of Tondo and Maynilad were established.

The arrival of Islam

Islam started to arrive in the far south of the Philippine islands, particularly the Sulu islands, from about the 13th century onwards, through Arab missionaries carried by Chinese ships from Indonesia and neighbouring Borneo. The first mosque known to have been built in the Philippines was established in Sulu by Makhdum Karim, an Arab trader, in 1380. The first Islamic sultanate was set up – also in Sulu – in 1457 by Shari'ful Hashem Syed Abu Bakr, an Arab born in Johore, in today's Malaysia. At its peak the Sulu Sultanate covered not just the Sulu islands, but also those islands immediately around Mindanao, parts of Borneo, and Palawan to the north.

The formation of the Sultanate of Sulu was followed in 1527 by the establishment of the Sultanate of Maguindanao in western Mindanao, while at about the same time Tondo and Maynilad came under Islamic rule when they became part of the Kingdom of Brunei.

The arrival of the Spanish

The Spanish chapter in the Philippines' history began in 1519, when the Portuguese adventurer Ferdinand Magellan began a commercial project on behalf of the Spanish crown. Setting sail from Spain with five ships, he aimed to find a route to the Spice Islands (now Indonesia) by sailing westwards, instead of the more usual eastward route around Africa. His journey led him to explore the southern coasts of South America, eventually finding a route around its southern tip, through what is now known as the Straits of Magellan.

From here he sailed across the Pacific Ocean, in March 1521 reaching the east coast of the Philippines, his flotilla by this time reduced to three vessels. Upon making landfall, not only did he claim the islands for Spain, but he also led the first mass to be held on Philippine soil. The exact location is often disputed, though Limasawa Island, off the southern tip of Leyte is most often credited. From here he was directed to Cebu, as the commercial hub for this part of the archipelago.

At Cebu he initially received a rather cautious welcome, though Magellan soon won over the local principal chieftain, Rajah Humabon, even persuading him to convert to Christianity. It was at Humabon's baptism that Magellan presented the gift of the Santo Nino, the statue of Christ as a child, much treasured today by religious Filipinos and housed in the Basilica Minore del Santo Niño in downtown Cebu City.

Being the area's most senior leader, Humabon's conversion to Christianity put neighbouring subordinate chiefs under pressure to follow suit. Lapu-Lapu, chieftain on the nearby island of Mactan refused to convert. Magellan felt compelled to assert his authority, and on 27th April 1521 he moved in to attack Lapu-Lapu despite

Above: Magellan's Cross, in Cebu City, supposedly marking the site where Ferdinand Magellan baptized the local paramount chief Rajah Humabon in 1521.

being hugely outnumbered. Muskets were no match for the sheer number of men sent against the Spaniards, and during the struggle it is said that Lapu-Lapu himself killed Magellan. Today, he is hailed as the first great patriot to resist foreign invasion.

Humabon's own men then set upon the surviving Spaniards, who not surprisingly fled aboard their ships. They did eventually reach the Spice Islands, and two years after fleeing the Philippines the last few survivors – 18 men out of an original 265 – made it back to Spain. Despite the tragedy, the voyage was a momentous achievement, the first ever known circumnavigation of the Earth, and the establishment of a new trade route between Europe and Southeast Asia.

The Manila Galleons

One of Spain's main aims in taking over the Philippines was the establishment, control and monopolization of trade between the region and Spain. Thus, the Philippines became locked into a trade monopoly with Spain, administered from Mexico, which from the middle of the 17th century up to 1815 took the form of two annual ships, each travelling in opposite directions, crossing the Pacific between Manila and Acapulco, on Mexico's west coast.

Called the Manila Galleons, the ship bound for Mexico carried Oriental goods that were in huge demand in Europe and Mexico, particularly Chinese ceramics and silk, Indonesian spices, carpets and artworks, all paid for in Mexican silver dollars aboard the westbound ship. It was a lucrative trade, enriching Manila's Spanish and mixed-race 'Mestizo' population.

It also enriched the city's Chinese, who found themselves at the very heart of the trade, the Spanish completely dependent on their network of contacts stretching right across Southeast Asia. Without them, it would have been far harder to bring the region's rich cornucopia to Manila. Inevitably, this gave them a power that made the Spanish highly suspicious, and when the Chinese eventually rebelled they were banished from ever entering Intramuros and were forced to live in a riverside area called the Parian, within range of the Spanish cannons.

The colonial authorities did eventually relent a little, however. Those Chinese who converted to Christianity were allowed to settle in an area called Binondo, on the north bank of the Pasig River, an area that to this day is at the centre of Manila's Chinatown, a busy, if somewhat rundown and overcrowded commercial district.

The Manila Galleons trade went into decline in the late 18th century following the creation of the Royal Philippine Company, which shipped goods directly to Spain via the Cape of Good Hope, and the galleons' crossings eventually came to an end in 1815.

Spain tightens its grip

Things moved rather slowly for quite some time after that. Two more expeditions investigated the islands, the leader of the second Ruy Lopez de Villalobos, coining the name Islas Filipinas in honour of the then Spanish king, Philip II.

It was the third expedition, however, that began the Spanish colonization of the Philippines, led by Miguel Lopez de Legazpi. He landed in Cebu in 1565, quickly taking control of the port, and establishing Fort San Pedro and the Philippines' first Spanish settlement. However, this was soon moved to Iloilo on the island of Panay as a defensive measure against a feared attack by the Portuguese. Searching for a permanent site for his capital, Lopez de Legazpi decided to investigate reports he had received of major trading centres situated further north at Tondo and Maynilad.

In May 1570 he dispatched a fleet of ships to the north. The fleet's commander, Martin de Goiti opened negotiations with Rajah Soleiman, chief of Maynilad, a process that ended in the Spanish ships bombarding Maynilad into surrender. The fleet then returned to Panay to report back to Lopez de Legazpi. He clearly liked what he heard, for in June 1571 he returned with his fleet. This time Soleiman and his citizens did the job for the Spaniards, burning Maynilad to the ground themselves, before fleeing. The citizens of neighbouring Tondo proved much more cooperative, quickly agreeing terms with Lopez de Legazpi.

Spanish Manila grew up on the site of Maynilad, initially a wooden settlement, but as a result of repeated pirate attacks soon becoming the heavily fortified stone city, known as Intramuros, that we see today. Subsequently one of Lopez de Legazpi's commanders, Juan de Salcedo, extended control to the far north of

Above: An entrance to one of the bastions, a Spanish-era fortress guarding the walls that surround Intramuros, the old Spanish capital.

Luzon, establishing a new base at the northwest coastal town of Vigan. To this day, Vigan retains a Spanish quarter, lovely streets of Castilian houses that have gained the town UNESCO World Heritage Site status.

Administered from Mexico, the Spanish began their total takeover of the Philippines. Priests set about converting the population en masse to Catholic Christianity, while at the same time ensuring the almost total destruction of everything relating to the pre-Hispanic period, from animist religious artefacts, through musical instruments and styles, to even the alphabet. Their work ensured that from there on the people were exposed only to European, and particularly Spanish, influences. Meanwhile, to ensure easier control and monitoring of the population, the traditionally diffusely spread barangays were compressed into distinct villages and towns built around a church. The Encomienda system, originally set up in the South American colonies, was also established in the Philippines. This was a system whereby entire packages of land and everything on it (including the people) were awarded to Spaniards who had faithfully served the Spanish crown. Inevitably, it led to massive exploitation and absentee landlordism. It also resulted in the concentration of land, and hence power, into the hands of a very small elite; a problem that persists to this day, despite repeated promises by successive governments to bring about reform and a more equitable distribution of land ownership.

Resistance to Spanish rule

From the earliest days of colonial rule, rebellions were not uncommon. The Spanish were never able to fully extend their control over the tribes of mountainous northern Luzon, which is why these people have retained so many of their traditions – and their independent spirit – to this day. In the far south, there was constant conflict with the Moslems, where – as with the mountainous north – Spain never gained full control and for example, only managing to capture the city of Jolo, in the Sulu archipelago, during the second half of the 19th century.

Operating within an area of northern Luzon under full Spanish control, two of the most renowned rebels were husband and wife team Gabriela and Diego Silang, who ran a successful guerrilla war for many years during the 18th century, and which was continued by Gabriela long after her husband was killed in fighting. She was eventually captured, tortured and executed, however Gabriela has lived on in the country's history as the first Filipina heroine, immortalized in a statue that stands close to the Stock Exchange in Metro Manila's modern Makati business district. Perhaps the most successful of all rebels was Francisco Dagahoy, who led a revolt on Bohol Island in 1744, and which gave the island independence for over 80 years before it was finally retaken by the Spanish in 1829.

Revolution

With the opening up of the Philippines to a wider world, as well as the increasing numbers of anti-Spanish rebellions in South America, 19th century ideas of freedom and democracy began to permeate into the country via those Filipinos able to travel abroad. Prominent among these was José Rizal, a young doctor who studied medicine in Madrid as well as a number of other European countries. He began to write increasingly about self-

Above: The Rizal Monument, memorializing José Rizal, father of the nation, standing in Rizal Park, Manila, close to the spot where he was executed in 1896.

determination for the Philippines, most notably through two novels 'Noli me Tangere' and 'El Filibusterismo'. Not surprisingly, his work was banned in the Philippines, and when he returned to the country he was exiled to Mindanao. Despite this, his work clearly had an impact, and today he is widely revered as the father of the Philippine nation, his statue adorning the central squares of almost every village, town and city across the country.

While Rizal favoured a peaceful approach to the goal of Philippine independence, others advocated the violent overthrow of colonial rule. At the forefront of this movement was Andres

Bonifacio, who in 1875 established the 'Katipunan', an underground movement dedicated to revolution. In just a few years the movement grew from a few hundred members to tens of thousands, and in 1896 when the Spanish eventually discovered and attacked the movement Bonifacio was forced to launch the revolution.

At this point the Spanish brought Rizal back to Manila, where he was tried and then executed outside the walls of Intramuros, in what is now Rizal Park. He was shot on 30th December 1896, aged just 35. The Philippine Revolution was handed its first martyr.

In the Katipunan in-fighting started to interfere with the war against Spain, culminating in the trial and execution of Bonifacio. He was replaced by General Emilio Aguinaldo, who subsequently led his men to a stalemate against the Spanish. Neither side could defeat the other, so in May 1897 a treaty was signed, ending the revolution and sending its leaders into exile in Hong Kong. The first attempt at independence had fizzled out.

The Americans arrive

Things did not stay peaceful in the Philippines for very long. In April 1898, the mysterious sinking of an American warship in Havana harbour during the Cuban uprising led to the Spanish-American War. The US encouraged the Filipino exiles to return home to start a new rebellion, Aguinaldo returning from exile and declaring Philippine independence on 12th June 1898, with himself as the first president. Meanwhile, the American navy attacked and sank the Spanish fleet in Manila Bay, and combined Filipino-American forces laid siege to Manila.

The Spanish opened negotiations with the Americans, agreeing to surrender only after a face-saving mock battle and only if the Filipino forces were excluded. The Americans agreed, persuading the Filipino soldiers to move aside to make way for US troops, before launching their 'attack'. The Spanish garrison surrendered on 13th August 1898, allowing an American takeover of the city, with the Filipinos frozen out of any further involvement.

Any doubts as to US intentions were dispelled by the Treaty of Paris, signed in December 1898, in which Spain agreed to sell the Philippines, Puerto Rico and Guam to the USA for $20 million. The Philippines were simply passed from one colonial master to another. Aguinaldo attempted to declare independence once again, but was met with no international recognition. Within months the Philippine-American War began.

It was probably rather a one-sided fight, and the war was ended in April 1902, following the capture of Aguinaldo and his subsequent oath of allegiance to American control. Although the war had ended across much of the country, in the Islamic south, the Americans, like the Spanish before them, found it very difficult to assert control. The war rumbled on across much of Mindanao and the Sulu islands until 1913, during which time the Americans were accused of a number of atrocities.

Despite early talk about the Philippines being given independence, the US displayed little inclination to release its hold on the country for a number of years. In the early 1930s however, it was finally agreed that the Philippines would at last gain independence, first passing through a semi-autonomous commonwealth phase, before gaining full independence in 1946. True to their word, the commonwealth was established on 4th July 1935, with Manuel Quezon as president. The path to full independence, however, was to take something of an unexpected detour.

Left: The Mindanao Peace Monument in Davao City, depicting an angel and dove, a priest, and members of Islamic and non-Islamic cultural groups, symbolizing the three ethnic and religious pillars of multicultural Mindanao.

The Japanese invasion

The Japanese attack on Pearl Harbor on 7th December 1941 changed everything, and was quickly followed by Japanese landings on the Philippines. The heavily outnumbered Filipino and US forces retreated to the Bataan peninsula and Corregidor Island, defendable locations on the opposite side of Manila Bay from the capital, where they made a last stand. The Philippine government and the US commander, General Douglas MacArthur, were evacuated, and by May 1942 their forces had surrendered to the Japanese invaders. The Philippines had a third colonial master.

Japanese rule lasted three years before MacArthur returned in October 1944 landing American troops at Red Beach on Leyte. Several more landings followed elsewhere in the Philippines, and in January 1945 Manila was retaken after heavy fighting that saw much of the city reduced to rubble. Few of the historic buildings in Intramuros survived: most of what is seen inside the walls today is a post-war reconstruction.

A new nation is born

Despite the mayhem of the preceding years, the timetable to independence remained unchanged, the Philippines finally gaining its freedom after almost 400 years of colonial rule on 4th July 1946. Manuel Roxas was the first president, at the head of an American-style presidential government system backed by a two-house congress.

Although this was a momentous development for the Philippines, not everyone was entirely happy with the way things were going. During the Japanese occupation a number of resistance movements had sprung up, waging a guerrilla war against the invaders. The most successful of these was the Hukbalahap, or Huk for short, a communist group based in central and northern Luzon. They aimed not just to rid the country of the Japanese but also to destroy the land ownership system inherited from the Spanish encomienda system, which had resulted in huge estates being concentrated into a few hands.

They were very successful, and by the end of the war controlled large parts of northern Luzon, taking over most of the estates and redistributing the land amongst peasant farmers. The return of both the Americans and the Filipino ruling elite at the end of the war was an unwelcome return to the old system for the Huk, and when they were prevented from taking part in the government of the newly independent country they returned to their guerrilla warfare, launching a rebellion that ran from 1946 until 1954.

The rebellion was quite successful, and it is often said that in 1950 the Huk almost captured Manila. However, when this was followed by American assistance to the government the tables were turned. In 1954 the last of the Huk's leaders surrendered and the rebellion was over.

Top: A statue of General MacArthur wading ashore at Red Beach, Leyte, memorializing the American landings that helped to free the Philippines from Japanese occupation.

Above: The ruins of barracks on Corregidor Island in the mouth of Manila Bay, site in 1942 of the last stand for American and Filipino troops against the invading Japanese.

Opposite above: American troops aboard a ship, fighting off Japanese aircraft during US landings on Mindoro, February 1945.

Opposite below: Filipino soldiers marching during Independence Day celebrations (12th June) in Manila.

The Philippines has remained closely allied to the Americans throughout its independence, allowing the US to maintain large military bases on its soil, particularly the vast Subic Bay naval base and the nearby Clark Air Force base, both in northern Luzon. These were hugely important during the Vietnam War, providing staging points for supplies and attacks, as well as an ideal location for troop R and R. In the late 1980s both these bases became a major sovereignty issue for the Philippines, and when they were severely damaged by ash fallout from the Mt Pinatubo eruption in 1991, during which they had to be evacuated, it became a simple matter for the US to withdraw. The bases finally closed in 1992. This did not mark the complete end of American military involvement in the Philippines, however. Since the 9/11 attacks in New York and Washington DC, the USA has given extensive assistance to the Philippines' struggle against its Islamic insurgencies.

The Marcos years

By the early 1960s, the Philippines' economy was booming, making it one of the strongest in Southeast Asia. The 1965 election saw a young Ferdinand Marcos elected president, modelled in something of a John F. Kennedy mould, and ushered in on a wave of optimism that he would bring about serious land reform, the perennial bugbear of rural Philippine life.

For the first few years Marcos was successful, leading to his re-election to a second term in 1969, though even then there were allegations of vote-rigging in his favour. The snails-pace of land reform, however, coupled with growing allegations of corruption, was taking the lustre off his leadership, leading to growing unrest. Marcos was also troubled by the formation of a new communist army, the New People's Army (NPA), and a resurgence of the south's Islamic rebellion. Barred by the constitution from standing for election for a third term, in 1972 Marcos used the unrest as an excuse to declare martial law, cancelling the constitution and replacing it with his own brand of parliamentary government to legitimize his usurpation of power.

The next 14 years saw Marcos and his cronies embezzle vast sums from the Philippine economy. Despite this, he was supported by the US government in exchange for his support in the anti-communism struggle. All opposition was stifled through arrest, exile or murder, although one opponent who struggled on was Benigno 'Ninoy' Aquino, a senator who had been groomed to stand in the presidential election due in 1973. Eventually, even he was forced into exile for his own safety. After just three years, in 1983, Aquino chose to return to lead the anti-Marcos struggle. Sadly, he was to lead it from his grave: Aquino was shot dead literally as he was stepping off a plane at Manila airport.

It was the beginning of the end for Marcos. Aquino's murder was followed by mass boycotts and general non-cooperation by the population, leading the economy to slide ever closer to bankruptcy. In 1985, Marcos – persuaded by the US – called snap elections, which were held on 7th February 1986. His opponent was Corazon Aquino, widow of Benigno, and spearhead of a united opposition. The official poll organizers declared Marcos the winner, but an independent election monitor cried foul, citing huge vote rigging and intimidation, and declared Aquino the winner. Parts of the Philippine military, led by Defence Minister Juan Ponce Enrile and Vice Chief of Staff Fidel Ramos, attempted to launch a military coup but failed, and at this point the hugely popular archbishop

The People Power Revolution

Also called the EDSA Revolution for the acronym commonly used for the name of the avenue on which most of the action took place, this revolution swept through Manila during the days of 22nd–25th February 1986 as a direct result of fraudulent elections run by the then president Ferdinand Marcos.

Desperate to be rid of the corrupt Marcos, who – as described in the main text – had held onto power through more than a decade of martial law, the opposition refused to accept the election result, insisting that their leader, Corazon Aquino, was the winner. Juan Ponce Enrile, then Minister of National Defence, and Lt Gen Fidel Ramos, Vice Chief of Staff, attempted to launch a coup from Camp Aguinaldo, a military base in the heart of Manila. When this failed, Cardinal Jaime Sin, archbishop of Manila and a long-time opponent of Marcos went onto the opposition's radio station, Radio Veritas, to call upon the people of Manila to take to the streets to protect the rebel soldiers.

Hundreds of thousands of people poured onto Epifanio de los Santos Avenue (EDSA for short), blockading the routes into Camp Aguinaldo and leading to such scenes as nuns praying in front of government tanks. The troops proved unwilling to open fire on unarmed civilians, and although tear gas was used in a few skirmishes, in general the army tended to pull back from confrontation with the demonstrators. More and more military units began to switch support to the opposition. Throughout the turmoil, Radio Veritas broadcast details of everything that was happening despite repeated attempts by government troops to shut it down.

On Monday 24th February, Marcos held a televised press conference, broadcast by government-controlled TV station Channel 4. However, the conference was never fully transmitted, the station going off-air halfway through when it was captured by rebel troops. The following morning Corazon Aquino was sworn in as president, and although Marcos declared himself as president, it was clear support for him both within the Philippines and internationally was rapidly evaporating. On the morning of Tuesday 25th February 1986 Ferdinand Marcos and his family were airlifted by American helicopters out of the Malacanang Palace, the presidential home, to Clark Air Force Base and thence to exile in Hawaii. After Marcos had left demonstrators quickly stormed and took over the palace.

The People Power Revolution had triumphed with hardly a single drop of blood spilled, and returned the Philippines to democratic government, with Corazon Aquino installed as president.

Opposite: Filipinos in Manila celebrating the installation of Corazon Aquino as president, following the February 1986 People Power Revolution.

of Manila, Cardinal Jaime Sin, made a radio appeal, calling for the people of Manila to take to the streets to protect the rebel soldiers.

Hundreds of thousands of people responded in what became known as the People Power Revolution (see box story), which culminated in US helicopters flying Marcos and his family out to exile in Hawaii. The Philippine people had triumphed in a largely peaceful revolution.

Democracy returns

Corazon Aquino was sworn in as president, but she proved to be an unskilled leader. The economy continued to struggle, there were numerous attempted military coups against her, and insurgencies multiplied around the country. The NPA started to gain control of large areas of the countryside in the north, while in the south two Moslem armies, the Moro National Liberation Front (MNLF) and the Moro Islamic Liberation Front (MILF) were gaining ground.

The 1992 election saw Aquino replaced by Fidel Ramos, who quickly made peace deals with the NPA and the MNLF, satisfying the latter with the creation of an autonomous Islamic area in western Mindanao and Sulu, though the MILF refused to support the agreement. He slowly put the economy back on its feet, launching a programme of industrialization and education, called Philippines 2000, which by the end of the decade had the economy growing faster than almost any other in Southeast Asia.

Unfortunately, in the 1998 election Ramos was replaced by Joseph Estrada, a popular film star who promised land reform and riches for all. He proved to be astonishingly inept and corrupt, undoing much of the progress achieved by Ramos, and in 2001 was ousted by another peaceful revolution, often dubbed People Power II, and replaced by his vice president Gloria Macapagal-Arroyo. Estrada was placed under house arrest for the next seven years, before finally being tried and convicted of corruption. He was jailed for life, but astonishingly was immediately pardoned by the president and released.

Gloria Macapagal-Arroyo has been president since 2001, winning another election in 2004. Her government has been reasonably successful, rebuilding the Philippines and once again making it one of the fastest growing economies in Southeast Asia. However, she has been increasingly accused of corruption, though how serious this corruption is in the context of unscrupulous previous governments remains to be seen.

Communist insurgencies now appear to be a thing of the past, but there was a huge increase in Islamic insurgency following September 2001, led by the MILF and a militant group, Abu Sayyaf. Both have been responsible for a string of guerrilla attacks, kidnappings, assassinations and bombings, continuing to maintain a volatile situation in southwest Mindanao.

Chapter Four

Government and Economy

Since independence in 1946, the Philippines has experienced a rollercoaster ride both in terms of its government and its economy. Cycles of boom and bust interspersed with a string of insurgencies, attempted coups, corrupt government leaders and natural disasters have repeatedly damaged the country. Time and again, outsiders and Filipinos alike have looked on in despair as a thriving economy, recovering well from the last disaster, grinds to a halt once again with the onset of the next. Through it all, however, the country has stuck to its hard-earned principles of democracy and free speech, generating a colourful press that is not shy in encouraging the national pastime of lampooning politicians, a piece of entertainment that has repeatedly exposed corrupt dealings.

Opposite above left: A dusk view of Manila's port.

Above: A complex mass of fish traps and levered nets create a serious obstacle course for fish in a river estuary on the west coast of Negros.

Opposite left: Newly planted and vibrantly green rice fields close to the village of Sagada, in the Cordillera Central mountains of northern Luzon.

Left: A grove of coconut palms, Dauin, near Dumaguete, Negros.

Government and Economy

"The government structure is modelled very much on the American system, headed by a powerful elected president…"

Underpinning the political and economic system is one major structural issue that has been an integral part of the Philippines since the Spanish colonial era, and which has defined both government and the economy since the first days of independence. It is the unequal distribution of land and power, with vast estates concentrated in the hands of a small number of people – who inevitably largely form the country's ruling elite – leaving huge numbers of rural poor struggling to find either sufficient land to farm or sufficient work to bring in an income. It is an issue that virtually every incoming Philippine government has pledged to try to solve and yet one which still remains a critical problem and a dilemma which lies behind just about every one of the numerous communist uprisings that have ripped through the country over the past half-century. Solving this thorny issue remains arguably the greatest challenge for the Philippines' leaders, both politicians and business chiefs.

Governing the Philippines

The government structure is modelled very much on the American system, headed by a powerful elected president aided by a cabinet that he or she appoints, backed by a two-house congress of elected representatives. The president is chosen by national elections every six years, and since the debacle of the Marcos years is allowed to serve only a single term.

As with the USA, Congress consists of two houses, the Senate and the House of Representatives, the former the upper house. In the Philippines, the Senate contains 24 senators, who serve for six-year terms, with half standing for election every three years,

elected by a national vote. The House of Representatives contains a maximum of 250 members, 206 elected to represent single-seat geographical areas, the remaining 44 from sectors of society, elected via a complex 'party list' system. At present there are only 238 representatives. Members of the House of Representatives are elected every three years, with no one allowed to serve more than three consecutive terms.

Unlike the USA, the Philippines is not a federal country, but is run as a single entity, divided into 17 regions, including one autonomous region. Below the regional level the country is divided into 80 provinces, which themselves are subdivided into cities, municipalities and barangays. The barangay is the smallest unit of local government, working at the local community level, which in a city usually equates to a district, and in the countryside to a village. Each level of government has an elected leader (provincial governor, mayor and barangay captain) and an elected assembly.

The one autonomous region is the Autonomous Region in Muslim Mindanao (ARMM), created in 1990 as part of a peace deal with the separatist Moro National Liberation Front (MNLF). It consists of four provinces in western Mindanao (Lanao del Sur, Maguindanao, Basilan and Tawi-Tawi) plus the Sulu archipelago. It has the power to raise its own taxes and run its own internal affairs, but is allowed no role in defence and international relations, and recognizes the overall authority of the Manila government.

At the time of ARMM's creation, a much larger area was balloted in a general referendum, but only the four Mindanao provinces listed above voted to join, with Sulu joining later. In 2008, a peace deal with one of the remaining Moslem rebel groups, the Moro Islamic Liberation Front (MILF), added new areas to ARMM, but following protests from residents living within those areas the Supreme Court ruled the extension illegal due to the lack of any public consultation.

Political parties

The Philippine political scene is characterized by a bewildering array of political parties, whose allegiances and policies seem to change with astonishing ease and frequency, making it very difficult to keep up with latest developments! At election time the popular vote can easily become fragmented, as a result of which even the biggest parties generally have to form coalitions, even before the elections, in order to secure a chance of gaining power.

Prominent among these is the Lakas-Kabalikat ng Malayang Philipino-Christian Muslim Democrats (abbreviated to Lakas-

Above: A freighter heads seawards from the port at Subic Bay. Until 1992, a major US naval base, Subic Bay is now an important industrial centre.

Kampi-CMD), a party formed in 2008 by the merger of Lakas-CMD and Kampi. The latter was formed only in 1998, while the former has been a major player in Philippine politics and government since the People Power Revolution, having two presidents elected from its leadership, Fidel Ramos in 1992 and Gloria Macapagal-Arroyo in 2004. Opposing Lakas-CMD-Kampi is the Genuine Opposition (GO), a major coalition at least during senate elections in 2007, an umbrella group that serves as government opposition, and which is a coalition of no less than eight parties.

Other important parties or groupings include the Nationalist People's Coalition (NPC), the Labang ng Demokratikong Pilipino ('Struggle of Democratic Filipinos'; LDP) and the Liberal Party (LP), all of which have been involved with important government or opposition coalitions in recent years, and which retain significant numbers of representatives in Congress.

Despite the strong party political tradition, when it comes to securing votes political doctrine and policies tend to take a back seat to the strength of individual personalities and their regional origins; something that explains the ease and speed with which politicians shift their loyalties as they attempt to align themselves with the most charismatic leaders. This love among the electorate of personality over policy was well illustrated by the disastrous 1998 election to the presidency of popular and charismatic film star Joseph Estrada, which ended in 2001 with the People Power II Revolution and Estrada's arrest for corruption. As for the much-maligned Ferdinand Marcos, even he is still greatly revered in his homeland area in the far northwest of Luzon.

Opposite: A dusk view of the port of Manila. Although accessible only to relatively small ships, the port is a vital conduit for the Philippines' exports.

The economy

Over the years, the state of the Philippine economy has closely reflected the state of the country's democracy. During the first 20 years of independence the economy grew steadily. By the early 1960s the Philippines had one of the strongest economies in East Asia and according to many reports second only to Japan. However in 1972 the declaration of Martial Law by Ferdinand Marcos was swiftly followed by his rapacious plundering of the Philippine economy. By the time he was finally ousted in 1986 the country was virtually bankrupt, and in terms of economic development left well behind by what would soon be known as the Asian Tiger economies of other Southeast Asian countries.

Since then, the country's economy has recovered well, apart from a temporary set-back during the period of Estrada's presidency and even weathering the Asian economic downturn of the late 1990s. Since 2001, the economy has been growing by about 6 per cent annually, outstripping most of its Asian neighbours, and reaching over 7 per cent shortly before the start of the global recession in 2008. Since then, growth has remained around 4.6 per cent, despite falling industrial production and hence exports.

Despite these improvements, the country's wealth still lags behind that of its neighbours, at least partly a result of it being bedevilled by the problems of a poor, under-employed and constantly growing rural population heavily dependent on agriculture for survival, let alone prosperity. Nationally, the average annual family income is just US$2900, but almost half of the population earns less than US$2 per day.

Interestingly, although agriculture contributes less than 14 per cent of today's economy in terms of the country's gross domestic product (GDP), it nevertheless employs about a third of the country's 36 million-strong workforce, dominating the lives of the impoverished rural population. Unfortunately, agriculture is the one sector of the economy struggling to improve output, at least in part due to environmental limits as well as economic ones, bedevilled by inequitable land ownership.

Above right: A shanty town built out over water houses some of Manila's poorest residents.

Centre right: Manila's container port, silhouetted against the sunrise, lies close to the city's Tondo district just north of the mouth of the Pasig River, and is crucial to the country's industrial output.

Below right: A mining engineer examines a zinc- and copper-containing rock at a mine on Rapu-Rapu Island.

Industry

Over half of GDP is generated by the service sector (including government), which employs roughly half the workforce. Significantly industry accounts for over a third of GDP, even though it employs only about 15 per cent of the workforce. Ever since the presidency of Fidel Ramos (1992–98), industrial development has been the main hope in generating wealth for the country as a whole and also employment for the poorer parts of society.

The programme of industrialization launched by Ramos was called Philippines 2000 and it went a long way to help the economy recover from the Marcos years, and similar initiatives have been continued by Macapagal-Arroyo. This industrialization, consisting largely of food processing, textiles and garment manufacture, as well as motor parts and electronics production (such as mobile phone chips), has been largely responsible for the growth in the economy. However, the new industries have mainly concentrated in central Luzon and around Metropolitan Manila in particular, with a lesser concentration around Cebu City. This has exacerbated the steady flow of people from the regions towards Metro Manila, whose population has grown by two million in just the past ten years and which now stands at almost 12 million.

Mining is traditionally a major Philippine industry, the country's volcanic mountains rich in copper, gold, silver, nickel and chromite, with smaller amounts of zinc, iron, manganese, cobalt and coal. Based on past production and proven reserves the Philippines is known to be the world's second richest source of gold and third richest for copper. The search for oil has so far produced little of value, though there is now widespread offshore prospecting in progress. Large reserves of natural gas have been found in and around Malampaya Sound, on the west coast of Palawan.

In recent years Philippine mining has rather languished in the doldrums at least in part due to a dispute over just how big a proportion of the mining operation foreign companies were allowed to own. Until 1995 that proportion was just 40 per cent but then a new law allowed 100 per cent foreign ownership. The legality of that new law was challenged, and it took another ten years for the Supreme Court to finally give the thumbs up to the 1995 legislation. Since 2005, a host of foreign mining corporations, particularly from China, Japan and Australia, have been lining up to pitch bids that will see billions of dollars invested in new mining ventures, the government claiming that it aims to attract US$6 billion for 23 new projects by 2010.

How the global recession that started in 2008 affects these plans remains to be seen, but even if some of the 23 new projects do not come to fruition, those that do are likely to have a dramatic impact on rural employment. That said, rural Philippines has sometimes suffered badly, in terms of environmental impacts, from mining – one of the most famous incidents being the 1996 pollution of rivers on the island of Marinduque by spillage from copper mine tailings – so a whole new programme of mining development might not be welcome without a comprehensive raft of enforceable environmental controls.

Overseas Filipinos and their remittances

The shortage of work and generally very low pay even when work is available has spawned a highly important sector of the Philippine economy: that of remittances sent home by Filipinos working overseas. Spread around the world and working in such areas as domestic service, catering, entertainment, construction and seafaring, the Philippine government's own statistics show there to be approximately two million Filipinos working overseas at any given time, although other sources say as many as 11 million Filipinos – about 12 per cent of the population – are abroad. Most work in Asia, particularly the Middle East which hosts over 40 per cent, and most especially in Saudi Arabia and the United Arab Emirates (UAE).

Known in the Philippines as Balikbayan or OFWs (Overseas Filipino Workers), many overseas Filipinos spend years working abroad – even if they have children back home – sending as much of their income as possible home to relatives. In places like Hong Kong they are generally seen as the back-bone of both the domestic service and catering/entertainment businesses, working as nannies and cleaners across many middle and upper class Hong Kong homes, and running many of the city's bars and nightclubs.

The amount of money they collectively remit is quite staggering. Government statistics showing it to run at about US$6–8 billion annually, making up as much as 25 per cent of the national GNP and outstripping foreign investment in the country!

Above: Overseas Filipinas, working in Hong Kong, relax in a group in the centre of the city on a Sunday, traditionally their day off.

Agriculture

Roughly 13 million people depend on agriculture either simply for a subsistence living, or for regular or seasonal employment on the plantations. The main commercial crops are rice, coconut and coconut products, maize (corn), pineapple, bananas and sugar cane. Although some of these, particularly rice, are grown on small family-owned farms, most are produced on a huge scale in large plantations owned by a relatively small number of people.

Rice is of course a major food staple for the Philippines, and as described in the box opposite makes up a huge proportion of the country's farmland. Of almost equal importance commercially is the coconut, 324 million coconut palms planted across about 3.1 million hectares (7.6 million acres), or about 25 per cent of the Philippines' farmland, the world's second largest area of coconut cultivation after Indonesia. An estimated 3.5 million farmers depend directly on the coconut, with a further 25 million indirectly reliant on its products. The enormous range of products possible, from the flesh and drink of the coconuts themselves, to the oils, fibres and timber, make for a very valuable and largely sustainable harvest that nets the country on average about US$6 billion annually in exports. Indeed, the Philippines is said to account for about 59 per cent of the world's total coconut exports, and in particular is the largest producer of coconut oil.

Sugar cane is produced on vast estates, mainly on the Visayan island of Negros, home to 202,000 hectares (499,000 acres) of the national total of 383,000 hectares (946,000 acres) of farmland given over to sugar. Nationally, about 40 million tonnes of sugar are produced annually, 22 million of those tonnes coming from Negros. Sugar has been produced in the Philippines since the 18th century, but it was not until the middle of the 19th century that its potential for large scale cultivation as an export crop was developed. This resulted in the creation of the huge sugar cane plantations, or haciendas, that typify the Negros landscape to this day. The hacienderos, as the owners are known, have accumulated huge wealth, and yet surveys have found that many repeatedly pay their workers (many of which are only seasonal) below the set minimum wage, exacerbating and exemplifying the huge gulf that still exists between the wealthy landowners and the rural peasant labourers.

Although sugar cane remains a major crop, it is now far less significant than it once was. In the 1950s and 60s sugar accounted for as much as 20 per cent of national exports, at least in part due to the protection it enjoyed through import quotas to the USA. Once this ended in the 1970s, coupled with falling international sugar prices, and general deregulation and improved production efficiency in such countries as Thailand and Australia, Philippine sugar sales and cultivation tumbled, and today much of its sugar production is used within its borders.

Essential rice

As with much of Asia, rice is the basic staple food of the Philippines, each person consuming an average of 100 kg (220 lb) of rice per year, accounting for 41 per cent of calorie and 31 per cent of protein intake. Not surprisingly, rice is the Philippines' principal crop, about 15 million tonnes being produced annually, accounting for about 4.27 million hectares (10 million acres), or about a third of the country's farmland.

Rice cultivation is spread across the entire country, though the main growing areas are the flat lands of central Luzon and the Cagayan valley of northern Luzon. Cultivation is divided almost equally between wet, paddy field rice grown during the wet season, and upland dry field cultivation during the dry season. In northern Philippines the former stretches from June to November and the latter November to May/June. In the south of the country this is reversed.

Unfortunately, the Philippines is unable to produce all the rice it needs, having to import about 10 per cent of demand, most coming from Thailand or Vietnam, making it one of the world's biggest rice importers.

This makes the Philippines particularly vulnerable to rising rice prices, as has been happening over the past few years, rising global demand and spiralling oil prices driving wholesale rice prices up from US$200–400 per tonne in 2007, to about US$700 per tonne in 2009. Concerned that rising rice prices could spark social unrest among the poor, the Philippines government has been attempting to stockpile imported rice to head off any further international price hikes.

Worse still, with the Philippines' population constantly expanding, predictions indicate that by 2020 the country will need about 40 per cent more rice than it does now. This is a problem around the world of course, and it is the work of the International Rice Research Institute (IRRI), which happens to be based in the Philippines, at Los Banos to the south of Manila, to constantly research ways to improve rice yields. The IRRI was at the forefront of the Green Revolution of the 1960s and 70s, when new strains of common crops, including rice, brought about huge increases in yields around the world. The same kind of revolution is needed again.

In 2009 the IRRI released three new rice strains, one salt-tolerant, the second flood-tolerant and the third drought-tolerant. The first is of importance to farmers in low-lying coastal areas, the second for wet season lowland cultivation, and the third for upland dry season growth, all three showing greatly improved production compared to standard strains. Also of growing importance in the Philippines are hybrid rice strains, which have been shown to generally produce about six tonnes of rice per hectare compared to 4.5 tonnes per hectare for standard strains (2.4 and 1.8 tonnes per acre, respectively).

Above: A man planting out rice seedlings in paddy fields near Loboc, Bohol. With machinery too expensive, this is a very labour-intensive task that often involves many members of a community.

Opposite above: A typical rural view, a farmhouse standing on the edge of field of nearly ripe rice, backed by a grove of coconut trees, seen at Palanan, northeast Luzon.

Opposite centre: A family living aboard a platform far from land, on a seaweed farm in shallow water over Arena Reef, Sulu Sea.

Opposite below: Fishermen landing an early morning catch of tuna, Camiguin Island, Mindanao. Most fishing around the Philippines is a subsistence livelihood that is struggling to keep up with a growing population.

Fishing is mainly seen as a subsistence livelihood, not attracting much by way of large scale commercial exploitation, but instead carried on by vast numbers of poor coastal dwellers, who depend on a daily catch for a very modest living. Unfortunately, overfishing and unsustainable practices, such as the use of dynamite and cyanide, over the past 25 years have had a dramatic effect on fish stocks, as well as greatly damaging the coral reefs, leading to a reduction in the amount of sustainable habitat available. In turn, declining fish yields are having a serious impact on the standard of living of many coastal communities, further impoverishing an already poor sector of society. Conservation measures, such as the creation of local no-fishing reserves, have started to have a positive impact on fish yields in some areas, but until this can be extended to a nationwide coastal fish conservation programme, the future does not look good for hundreds of thousands of Filipino fishing families.

Chapter Five

Daily Life and the Arts

Life in present day Philippines is an amazing hotchpotch of historic influences. This is true in both day-to-day activities and also in the nation's many arts. Malay, Chinese, Spanish and American inputs, from musical styles to surnames to language to food and to religion have all been thrown together in a huge cultural blender, spun around a few times and then spat out again as something uniquely Filipino, with almost nothing rejected as unacceptably foreign.

The result is a country that is unmistakably Southeast Asian, and yet which is quite comfortable with the widespread adoption of Spanish Christian names and surnames, the almost wholesale usage of a foreign language, namely English, in daily business and government and a long-running love affair with the razzamatazz and supposed luxury lifestyle promised by the rather nebulous idea of the 'American Dream'.

Opposite above left: An Islamic dance, from the Philippines' rich heritage of dance styles, being performed at a free performance in Rizal Park, Manila..

Opposite above centre: A motorized tricycle at Moalboal, Cebu, serves as an affordable form of taxi for local transportation.

Above: A blast of colour on the front of a jeepney, the quintessentially Filipino type of minibus used mainly for local public transport.

Opposite left: The 16th century statue of the Black Nazarene, surrounded by a huge crowd as it makes its annual tour of Quiapo, in Manila, during the Festival of the Black Nazarene.

Left: Piles of mangoes on show in a fruit market in Manila.

Daily Life and the Arts

"What makes women's prominence possible in today's society is the strength of the extended family…"

The cultural medley is quite apparent in daily life the moment you arrive in the Philippines, with the widespread ability of the population to speak quite high quality English. The compulsory teaching of English from a young age since the very beginning of the American colonial period has firmly embedded the language into Philippine society. Moreover, in a country characterized by a host of regional languages and dialects (as described in Chapter Two), one universal tongue is required to enable the nation to communicate adequately with itself; a tongue that is politically neutral and free from the implication that one ethnic group dominates the others. As a foreign tongue, even though belonging to one of the former colonial masters, English fulfils that neutral all-embracing role. As a result, English is the predominant language in government, and not surprisingly is also used extensively in many businesses. This does present something of a barrier to advancement for poorer, less well educated people, whose grasp of English is often not good enough for such advanced usage.

Inevitably, the English spoken by Filipinos is often not the same as that spoken by native speakers of the language, if only in terms of general pronunciation and accent. As a result, there can still be a barrier of misunderstanding between Filipinos and foreign visitors, even when both are speaking English, a barrier that frustratingly increases the further you travel from Manila. Furthermore, Filipinos increasingly mix English and one or more of the local languages, usually Tagalog, together into the same sentences, creating a hybrid language often called 'Taglish'.

Related to language, the cultural mix is very well illustrated by the diversity of names. Although Malay-type names are frequently heard throughout the country, English and most especially Spanish names are also widespread. In the case of the latter, names were more or less assigned by the Spanish authorities to overcome problems associated with the fact that pre-Hispanic Philippine society apparently had no surnames. To overcome the confusion of Filipino names, it is said that the authorities simply created a list of Spanish names they deemed appropriate and then applied them en-bloc in alphabetical order, starting with A in the north and

Above: A party, mainly of women, at Independence Day celebrations in Manila. Women in the Philippines play prominent roles in society.

working through the alphabet whilst advancing southwards. The result today is a continued widespread use of Spanish names, even though their bearers have not one molecule of Spanish blood in them, nor any knowledge of a single word of the language.

One highly significant feature of daily life that is not typical across much of East Asia and which may have its roots deep in pre-Hispanic society is the predominance of women. The fact that the country has had two women presidents in the past 25 years (Corazon Aquino and Gloria Macapagal-Arroyo) is just the beginning: women are prominent throughout business as well as government, achieving far higher status than is generally possible in the Philippines' neighbours. This could be seen as something of a spin-off from the American colonial era, but it is more likely to date from pre-Hispanic Philippines, when the largely animist society tended to assign spiritual and economic power to women, the men taking the lead in political and military life.

What makes women's prominence possible in today's society is the strength of the extended family; the support of older members of the family making it relatively straightforward even for mothers to go out to work. This is further aided by the inequalities in society that make it quite inexpensive for better off families to recruit nannies to look after children, again allowing mothers to work while also providing employment for women from poorer families.

As already described in Chapter Two, Catholic Christianity is hugely important in daily life for most Filipinos, with only 10 per cent of the population following other religions, mostly Islam, and a small percentage following animist beliefs. Animism, a belief in powerful spirits throughout much of the natural world, is not just about belief in animals but also in inanimate objects such as rocks. Animism predates both Christianity and Islam in the Philippines, and was probably followed by virtually the entire population before the arrival of other forms of religion. Today, open practise of animism is confined to some of the tribal minorities, particularly those of the Cordillera Central and Sierra Madre mountains of northern Luzon, as well as some groups in Mindanao.

However, although Christianity and Islam have almost completely supplanted animism throughout the rest of the population, some ghosts of that pagan past still linger on as a folk religion, even among the most devout Catholics. Superstition and a general belief in spirits and witchcraft are still widespread, coupled with support for the use of herbal concoctions to break and create spells. This is coupled with a wide range of herbal remedies for a host of medical and non-medical conditions, remedies that are sometimes claimed to cure not through any pharmacological route but through their effects on good and evil spirits. Bottles of such remedies can be seen for sale in markets across the country.

Getting around

Even the simple act of travelling around takes on a classically Philippine look. While buses are the norm for long-distance journeys, for getting around cities, towns and some remoter rural areas the jeepney is king. Utterly unique to the Philippines, the jeepney was born at the end of the Second World War when the country suffered a chronic shortage of public transport but an excess of abandoned American military jeeps. Mechanics set to work cutting the jeeps in half, extending their chassis, adding long benches down each side of the now quite long jeeps, and throwing a roof over the whole lot. The jeepney was born.

Things have come a long way since those early days. Those early jeepneys represented a blank canvas for pop art, and the artists have really gone to work with a vengeance. Today's jeepney is now a mass of shiny metal, largely covered with a blaze of colour, in patterns, pictures, flashing coloured lights and even statuettes, topped off with an extremely powerful music system. Though excruciatingly uncomfortable, especially when crowded, and in Manila at least these days in competition with air-conditioned 'tamaraw' minibuses, the jeepney remains the workhorse of the local public transport system right across the country.

Jeepneys may not always get you where you want to go, or may not be the best form of transport. Then you need some form of taxi. Although taxis are common in the big cities, in many parts of the country cars are generally too expensive for many would-be taxi drivers to buy or would require rates too high for many people to be able to hire them. The solution is the motor tricycle, a motorbike with seating, a third wheel and a canopy clamped to one side. Not wonderfully comfortable or rain-proof, they are nevertheless a convenient method to get you and a companion or two from the bus station to hotel for example.

The universal jeepney and tricycle version of the Philippine seas is the *banca*, a long narrow canoe with wooden or bamboo outriggers on both sides to provide stability, with an inboard engine built into the main hull. Ideal for moving around in shallow, protected waters typically found around many of the islands. The *banca*'s very shallow draft means they have little trouble pulling right up to the shallows of a beach or in passing over a coral reef covered by even a limited amount of water. Be warned, though: in a lumpy sea those outriggers always kick up plenty of spray, resulting in a wet ride for anyone sitting in the wrong part of the boat!

Needless to say, although an engine is almost universal in the *banca* these days, originally it was powered by a single large sail, which can still sometimes be seen, a type of *banca* commonly called a 'paraw'. The motorized *banca* is sometimes given another name in English – a pump boat – so named due to the regular need to pump it out, a result of the universal and incurable leak that occurs around the engine's drive shaft as it passes through the bottom of the hull!

Above: A spectacularly shiny and colourful jeepney, a piece of public transport 'pop-art'.

Food

Nowhere is the Philippines' eclectic mix of influences more clearly illustrated than in its food. As with most East Asian countries, rice is a basic staple, but it is in the preparation of dishes to go with the rice that shows up the mix of influences, largely Southeast Asian, Spanish or Chinese. Unlike the rest of Southeast Asia, flavourings rarely go much beyond the use of salt, pepper and garlic, fiery chillies rarely having much place in Filipino meals, something that immediately creates a clear distinction from neighbouring Indonesia and Malaysia. In common with these countries, however, coconut milk is commonly used, giving a sweet, creamy taste and texture to those meals in which it is used.

Inevitably, seafood figures prominently, fish often being fried or steamed, served on a bed of rice with no other additions in a simple meal, or with a few vegetables in a more elaborate meal. Chicken and pork are also commonly used, less often beef and goat. The first two are frequently cooked in *adobo* style, a Spanish method of marinating and then stewing in vinegar, soy sauce and garlic. Pork is frequently served as *lechon*, a whole suckling pig roasted on a spit over a barbecue, a frequent meal at parties. A common soup-based meal is *sinigang*, a dish similar to the Thai *tom yam*, containing fish, shrimp, beef or pork as well as vegetables, with a rather sour taste caused by tamarind flavouring. Further Spanish influences come with its chorizo sausage and the paella rice dish, adapted into Filipino cuisine and called *longanisa* and *arroz valenciana*, respectively.

The Chinese influence appears frequently in the form of noodle dishes, either fried or as soups, while rice porridge is also not uncommon, interestingly often given the Spanish name *arroz caldo*. Popular snacks with Chinese origin are *lumpia*, large spring rolls, and *siopao*, doughy buns filled usually with either chicken or pork, but sometimes just vegetables.

Despite this vast range of Asian food, Filipinos have a great love affair with American fast food, and no high street is complete without a line-up of at least a few of the imported names, including McDonalds, Burger King, KFC, Wendy's, Dunkin Donuts and Pizza Hut, as well as a few home-grown versions, such as Jollibee.

As across much of Southeast Asia, sweet desserts are often made using sticky rice or rice flour. A very common and popular dessert frequently seen on sale in shops and cafes is *halo-halo*, essentially a bowl of shaved ice topped with milk and sugar, to which is added a range of ingredients, including coconut, purple yam, jackfruit, red beans or tapioca.

The availability of fruit does vary. Markets across the country are usually stocked with various types of bananas, apples and oranges, but surprisingly availability of many types of tropical fruit varies enormously with season and region. These include papaya,

Above and top: During Iloilo's annual Dinagyang Festival, held in January, the city's streets come alive with a food festival, featuring stalls selling a host of Philippine foods, especially a variety of grilled meats and seafood, as in these two images.

mango, rambutan, longgan, lychee, pineapple and mangosteen, but unfortunately poor distribution and difficulties with refrigeration mean that these are often not sold very far from their centres of cultivation. Coconuts can be remarkably difficult to buy: their wealth of economic uses makes them too valuable to simply sell in the market, and for rural people they are generally available for free whenever they want one.

Festivals

One of the greatest joys of Philippine life is the multitude of festivals that punctuate the year. Every town, city and village has its annual festival, either a religious event, a celebration of the annual harvest of the main local agricultural crop, the anniversary of a historical or mythological event, or a mixture of all three. Whatever the reason, the festival is the annual excuse to forget troubles and have a party, and if there is one thing Filipinos know how to do well it is to party.

A typical festival will consist of parades and competitions organized with varying degrees of professionalism and seriousness and all conducted in an atmosphere of loud music and much drunkenness. Most festivals, even non-religious ones, will usually have a religious element incorporated somewhere – such as the blessing of a local saint or statue – with beauty pageants also popular inclusions.

Of the religious festivals, arguably the most famous are the nationwide Good Friday events, particularly those in and around San Fernando in La Union province of northern Luzon, where participants willingly volunteer to endure brief periods of crucifixion, tied to – or sometimes even nailed to – a cross. Significantly less painful is the Festival of the Black Nazarene, held annually on 9th January in the Quiapo district of Manila. As mentioned in Chapter Two, the church here is renowned for its 16th century wooden statue of Jesus as a black man. During its festival the statue is paraded through Quiapo's narrow streets on a carriage pulled by teams of men. To merely touch the statue or the pulling ropes is to receive forgiveness for any sins, as a result of which the streets are thronged to near bursting point, the crowds in a constant struggle to reach the statue or to help pull it along.

Not surprisingly, it is a hopelessly chaotic scene, the statue often taking hours simply to cross the square in front of the church let alone get through the streets. Anyone wanting to watch this spectacle would be well advised to find a vantage point above the heaving crowd.

Another religious festival is Sinulog, taking place in Cebu City each January. This is the annual celebration of the city's greatest treasure, the 16th century statue of Santo Nino, Jesus as a child, given by Ferdinand Magellan to Hara Amihan, wife of Rajah Humabon, Cebu's chief, in 1521. The festival lasts for nine days, culminating in the Grand Parade, in which the statue is carried through the streets, followed by crowds in colourful costumes who perform a simple dance, supposedly unique to Sinulog, as they move through the streets.

Of the secular festivals, two of the most spectacular are Ati-Atihan and Dinagyang, both held in January on the island of Panay, in the cities of Kalibo and Iloilo, respectively. These are described in more detail in the box on page 63. Another popular festival is

Above: An elaborately costumed and choreographed tribal-style dance at Dinagyang Festival, in Iloilo.

The Ati-Atihan and Dinagyang Festivals.

These two festivals are a mixture of religious and secular events. Both are simultaneous celebrations of local Santo Nino statues – statues of Jesus as a child – and the anniversary of the 13th century agreement between the local Negrito people and the Ten Datus, Malay chiefs who had fled Borneo with their people. This agreement allowed these refugees to settle on Panay, forming the basis for much of the region's population today. Numerous other smaller festivals are conducted around Panay at this time to mark this anniversary, but all are much smaller than those in Kalibo and Iloilo.

Both festivals run for several days, and are a mixture of solemn religious processions and ceremonies, and riotous colourful affairs carried out in the cities' streets. The central feature of the street events is dance competitions among teams dressed in spectacular costumes; the winners decided on the basis both of their choreography and their costumes. In every case, the performers also blacken their skin with paint or soot to mimic the very dark skin of the Negritos. Ironically, the island's real Negritos take no part in the events.

Despite these similarities, Kalibo's Ati-Atihan and Iloilo's Dinagyang are very different events, the former a wild, uncontrolled affair in which participants and spectators mingle, while Dinagyang is very controlled and polished, each dance taking part in set places on the streets, surrounded by specially built spectator stands.

The two different styles will appeal to different people, but certainly anyone visiting the Philippines in January should make sure they get to at least one of the festivals, if not both.

Masskara, held every October in Bacolod, on the Visayan island of Negros. Dating from as recently as 1980, Masskara was born out of difficult times, when the region's economic mainstay, sugar, was selling at an all-time low price, and also shortly after a shipping disaster in which hundreds of Negros people had lost their lives. The festival was designed to lift Bacolod's depression, and since the city was known as the 'City of Smiling Faces', this has always been the festival's defining feature: participants are dressed not just in colourful costumes but also in masks that invariably depict a smiling face. As with Dinagyang and Ati-Atihan, a central feature is a competition among teams of colourfully dressed dance troupes, plus a carnival, beauty pageant, food festival, agricultural trade show and garden show.

On a much more serious note, 12th June sees the annual Independence Day celebrations, usually consisting of parades and speeches, a chance for the military to show off and for everyone to wave the flag.

Anyone visiting the Philippines for more than a couple of weeks is certain to run into at least one festival somewhere, whether it be a small village event or a massive national one, delivering a really good dose of local colour and action. There is only one rule – join in and enjoy the fun!

Above: A 'standard-bearer' for a tribal-style dance troupe at the Ati-Atihan Festival in Kalibo, Panay.

The arts

Four hundred years of colonial rule went a long way towards destroying indigenous art, replacing it with European ideas, coupled with an influx in the far south over several hundred years of Islamic styles. Starting in the early part of the 20th century, and most especially since independence, growing numbers of artists and academics have been busy piecing together the fragments to recreate a native pre-Hispanic style, particularly in dance and music.

Fortunately, the tribes of mountainous northern Luzon, who successfully resisted assimilation by the Spanish, have proved a valuable repository of pre-Hispanic styles, enabling at least a partial revival of traditional tribal instruments, music and dance.

As a result, Filipino music and dance now span four very different influences: indigenous pre-Hispanic tribal styles, Islamic Malay styles typical of Southeast Asia, classical European and particularly Spanish styles, and modern western, particularly American pop culture. In both the tribal and Islamic Malay styles, wind instruments consist of bamboo flutes, usually played with the mouth, though there are also nose flutes, used either singly or grouped together into panpipes; polyphonic clusters of different-sized pipes. Stringed instruments are wooden or bamboo zithers, lutes and fiddles. However, percussion is the most important instrument group, consisting of a wide collection of wooden drums and metal gongs.

Percussion is particularly important in the Islamic styles, where ensembles of metal gongs are responsible for the melody. Central to this style is the *kulintang*, a line of eight different sized gongs, each bearing a raised central boss, arranged in line on a wooden frame. The gongs themselves used to be made of bronze, but today are more likely to be made of brass, their different sizes and weights responsible for producing a wide range of tones when struck. The *kulintang* ensembles of the Philippines' far south are quite similar to the *gamelan* orchestras of neighbouring Indonesia and the *phiphat* of Thailand, Cambodia and Burma, illustrating not only the link with Indonesia, but also probably a pre-Islamic origin for these instruments.

Dance is of course closely linked to the music, both the tribal and Malay dances generally telling a story. Tribal dances, for example, are often about the important events in life, birth, death, marriage, the raising of children and farming. Among the most well known Malay dances are the *Tinikling* and *Singkil*, the latter portraying the Ramayana, one of the great Hindu epics, but both involving the dancers skipping their feet between bamboo poles that are rapidly clapped together. These dances can be seen not just in the far south of the Philippines, but in Borneo too. Inevitably, the hugely commercial American-influenced culture dominates the modern entertainment scene, threatening to swamp the traditional styles. Not only is American pop and rock music hugely popular, but they have spawned their own home-grown versions, known locally as OPM, (Original Philippine Music, or Original Pinoy Music). This has created a lively local music scene, generating a large pool of very talented musicians, many of whom these days make a living by working at nightclubs and hotels all over East Asia.

Rather more traditional are the high quality handicrafts widely available across the Philippines from souvenir shops to department stores, mostly produced by the indigenous tribes in northern Luzon and southern Mindanao. Fitting into three main categories, basketware, woodwork and textiles, most of the products represent items that may still be in common rural usage. Basketry is an obvious example of this, where products consist of a wide variety of fruit bowls, storage baskets, and mats, made mainly from such fibres as rattan and bamboo. Woodcarving is another popular tradition, most especially among northern Luzon's mountain tribes, who have adapted their skills from the carving of protective deity figurines. These include the *bulul*, the rice gods, effigies of which are frequently placed besides rice fields to protect the crop. Other wooden products include carvings of Christian saints and farm animals such as buffalo, and also quite elaborate furniture.

Textiles are produced, mainly by women, in many places around the country, using a variety of types of loom, producing a range of types of cloth with a host of patterns and colours. One typical traditional cloth is the *ikat*, very similar to cloth produced in Indonesia, hand spun, dyed using natural materials, and woven on a back-strap loom that generates strips up to 75 cm (30 in) wide and 3.5 m (11 ft) long. These days, almost all weaving uses cotton, though this was not introduced to some parts of the Philippines until the middle of the 19th century. Prior to that, fibres from banana, pineapple and abaca (hemp) plants were commonly used. In the remote Batanes islands, lying between northern Luzon and Taiwan, the fibres of the Voyavoy, a small palm tree, are still used to produce traditional rain capes, called *kanaye* for men and *soot* for women.

Above right: A performance of the *Tinikling*, a popular traditional dance that involves dancing with bare feet between two bamboo poles as they are rapidly clapped together.
Centre right: The Bayanihan national folk dance group performs an Islamic dance from the far south of the Philippines during an outdoor performance in Intramuros, Manila.
Below right: Although many dance influences are traditional, there is also considerable Spanish and some American input, as seen in this rather glittery vaudeville type of dance.

Chapter Six

Luzon, the Main Island

Luzon, you could say, is the Philippine heartland, the largest of the country's islands and home to the majority of the population. It is also the site of Manila, the nation's capital and economic engine. Luzon's landscape varies from high mountain ranges, the Sierra Madre, Cordillera Central and Zambales Mountains in the north, to a long narrow peninsula, known as Bicol, which stretches southwards for hundreds of kilometres and the location of a string of active volcanoes. These volcanoes range from Taal in the north, just south of Manila, to Mayon and Bulusan in the south.

Opposite above left: The spectacular pinnacle of Mt Mayon, the Philippines' most active volcano, towers over the city of Legaspi, in southern Luzon.

Above: A colourful and well-stocked fruit stall in San Andres market, in the Ermita district of Manila.

Opposite below: A sunset view of people relaxing on the seafront along Roxas Boulevard, in Manila.

Left: A forest ranger looks up at the giant buttress roots of a tree in lowland rainforest in the Subic Watershed Forest Reserve, Subic Bay, Luzon.

Luzon, the Main Island

Nationally important mountains in Luzon include Pulag, at 2930 m (9612 ft) the Philippines' third highest mountain, Mt Pinatubo, whose spectacular 1991 eruption was one of the largest and most destructive the world experienced in the 20th century, and Mt Mayon, the country's most active volcano, with almost 50 recorded eruptions. Along the coast, lie several clusters of remote islands, principally the Batanes and Babuyan Islands off the north coast, plus Polillo and Catanduanes off the east.

Pressure on the land for agriculture, logging, industry and housing has been intense and as a result environmental damage extensive, but some rainforest does survive, most notably the huge and extremely remote forests of the Sierra Madre, lining the northeast coast and shielded from the main body of Luzon by the Sierra Madre Mountains. Other forested areas include those at Subic Bay which are among the last stands of lowland rainforest in central Luzon, originally retained as a protective shield around the American Subic Bay Naval Base. Other protected forests survive on the slopes of Mts Makiling, Isarog and Bulusan, the first of these in the Calabarzon region immediately south of Manila, the last two in the Bicol peninsula.

Making up a third of the country's total land area, Luzon is home to over half its population with nearly 12 million crammed into the teeming streets of Metro Manila, one of Southeast Asia's biggest and most crowded cities. The majority of the population speaks Tagalog, the leading Filipino language and the native tongue of the Manila area, but other important languages include Pangasinan, Pampangan and Ilocano in the north and also Bicol in the south. The remote mountains of the north are home to quite a variety of tribal minorities, such as the Ifugao, Igarot, Bontoc and Kalinga, who resisted control by the colonial powers and still manage to maintain their own identities, including their own languages and religious beliefs.

For the visitor, Luzon's attractions hinge to some extent on the cultural sights of Manila's museums and the walled city of Intramuros, as well as the nightclubs and shopping of the Makati district. However, the main draw undoubtedly is the Cordillera Central, initially for its welcome breath of cool air after the humid tropical heat of the lowlands. More importantly, however, there is the draw of the tribal minorities' traditional lifestyles and skills, particularly the handiwork of the Ifugao's ancestors in building the mighty 2000-year-old rice terraces around the town of Banaue, as well as the Sagada people's traditions of cave burials.

Luzon's coasts are less of an attraction than those of the Visayan Islands further south, but a few hotspots would include the area around the fishing town of Donsol in the far south, where at certain times of the year it is possible to snorkel with whale sharks. The coral reef dive sites around Anilao, a little way south of Manila, the lovely rocky limestone islets of the Hundred Islands, near Dagupan and Luzon's busiest beaches at San Fernando are also worth a mention. The really adventurous might want to head off to the Batanes Islands, one of the country's remotest spots, lying midway between the northern tip of Luzon and Taiwan, for a taste of real island life and a truly traditional lifestyle.

Hikers will find a wealth of walking opportunities, mainly climbing the region's volcanoes, such as Taal, Makiling, Isarog and Banahaw, as well as Mayon and Bulusan (if eruption warnings allow!). The crowning glory is a hike to the summit of Mt Pulag, in the Cordillera Central, southeast of Baguio.

Opposite above left: The massive lake-filled crater of Mt Pinatubo, in the Zambales Mountains of northern Luzon, was created by the volcano's huge 1991 eruption.
Opposite above right: Mangroves and shoreline rainforest lit by the golden glow of early morning sunlight, in Triboa Bay, in Subic Watershed Forest Reserve, northern Luzon.
Opposite below: Emerald green rice fields surround the farmhouse of a family of Ifugao people, in Hapao, near Banaue, in the Cordillera Central mountain range of northern Luzon.

These pages: Farming is hugely labour-intensive, employing about a third of the country's workforce – mostly from the poorer parts of rural society – and yet contributing only about 14 per cent of the national economy. Equipment is generally quite primitive, requiring a lot of manual labour, as with this woman raking out her freshly harvested rice to dry, in southern Luzon (opposite top left). Despite this, the needs of rice cultivation at least, have led to some highly complex engineering feats, such as the creation of steep, mountainside terraces. Some of these are estimated to be 2000 years old and are now a UNESCO World Heritage Site, including those near the town of Banaue, in northern Luzon's Cordillera Central mountains (above). Many remote rural homes maintain their own smallholding plots, largely for subsistence purposes (opposite top right). Water buffalo are gentle giants that are essential in heavy agricultural work. When off-duty they love nothing better than to wallow in mud pools, an aid to cooling off during the hot sunshine; seen here in farmland near Legaspi, southern Luzon (opposite below).

These pages: At the start of the rice growing season, the young rice plants are nurtured in dense and vibrantly green nurseries, such as seen here in mountainside terraces near Banaue, before being planted out (above). Surrounded by fields of newly planted rice seedlings, a young boy heads to school along a path balanced along the top of a terrace (left). The steep mountains of the Cordillera Central range provide a verdant backdrop for this beautiful rural setting, near Banaue in northern Luzon. These rice terraces have been an essential part of the agricultural communities in this area for many hundreds of years. Though still cultivated, many are slowly falling out of use due to a steady drift of people to the cities.

This page: The Batanes Islands are one of the remotest regions of the Philippines, lying between Luzon and Taiwan, constantly lashed by the Pacific Ocean. Most of the population belong to the Ivatan cultural group, until very recently living a largely self-sufficient lifestyle. Traditional homes, still prominent on Sabtang Island, are solid stone structures with thatched roofs (left). Clothing woven from fibres of the Voyavoy palm is still made by hand (top left), worn by both men and women (above and above left).
Opposite page: It is a stunningly beautiful place, with a rugged but verdant coastline (opposite above). With their solid, rather rounded hulls, the islands' boats (opposite below) are adapted to local conditions, and are quite different from the narrow, outrigger-balanced craft typical of the rest of the country.

This page: The Philippines' wildlife is hugely diverse, and – due to the country's prolonged isolation from mainland Asia – quite distinct, with many unique, or endemic, species. The Rufous Hornbill, *Buceros hydrocorax* (top), is quite common, endemic to the Philippines, and easily seen in the forests of Subic Bay. The Luzon Bleeding-Heart Pigeon, *Gallicolumba luzonica* (above), is endemic not merely to the Philippines but actually just to Luzon, and is quite endangered. Colonies of the world's biggest fruit bats (right), often of mixed species, are not uncommon, seen here in the lowland rainforest of Subic Watershed Forest Reserve. These bats spend the day roosting in favourite trees in the forest, before heading out at night to feed on fruiting trees.

This page: The Rufous Night-heron, *Nycticorax caledonicus*, though common in mangroves is rarely seen since it is active mainly at dawn and dusk (above). The Reef Egret, *Egretta sacra*, is a solitary bird, quite commonly seen hunting for fish along many of the Philippines' shores (above left). An Anglehead Lizard, a large reptile almost a metre long, seen on a tree trunk in dense lowland rainforest at the foot of Mt Makiling, inside the Los Banos campus of the University of the Philippines (left). Reptile research is still at a relatively early stage and it is likely that as more species are discovered an even higher percentage will be found to be endemic.

These pages: With rapid change coming to many of the Ifugao people living in the mountains of northern Luzon, their traditional architecture is rapidly disappearing, thatched roofs, for example, giving way to corrugated zinc (above). At Hapao, a village near the town of Batad, an outdoor museum has preserved some of the traditional housing styles (top). Traditional clothing styles are disappearing too, but it is not difficult to find old men who will readily pose in their traditional clothing (left). Although the Ifugao are keen to cash in on the tourist market, they – along with other groups in these mountains – have long resisted attempts by colonial and Philippine powers to control them. As a result, they have a proud heritage that pre-dates the arrival of the Spanish, and which includes showing off their traditional weapons, textiles and styles of clothing.

Opposite page: Wherever there is water there is fishing, though in the Philippines usually at an individual or family level rather than on an industrial-type scale. Methods are often quite simple, including the now rarely seen bow-and-arrow method, demonstrated here by a Subic Bay Aeta tribesman (opposite left). As anywhere, nylon nets are widely used, as with this fishermen out at sunrise on Laguna de Bay (opposite below). In addition, permanently established fish traps and fish farms built using mainly bamboo are very common, particularly on lakes and river estuaries, as in this dawn view of Laguna de Bay (opposite right), just south of Manila. For many, fishing is largely a subsistence livelihood, and it has been reported that their poverty is increasing as over-fishing, pollution and habitat destruction take their toll on fish yields.

This page: The village of Sagada is a stunningly beautiful place high in the Cordillera Central mountains of northern Luzon, bathed in a cool temperate climate, surrounded by pine forests and karst limestone mountains, gorges and caves (top). The Sagada people, one of the region's cultural minorities, are renowned for leaving their dead in caves or even suspended from cliff faces, still commonly seen today (above). Much of the Philippines' revival of dance styles relies on traditional tribal themes, often derived from the peoples of northern Luzon's mountain regions (above right). The mountainous region of northern Luzon is well known for its colourful textiles, as promoted by the Easter School of Weaving, based in Baguio, the mountains' main city (right)

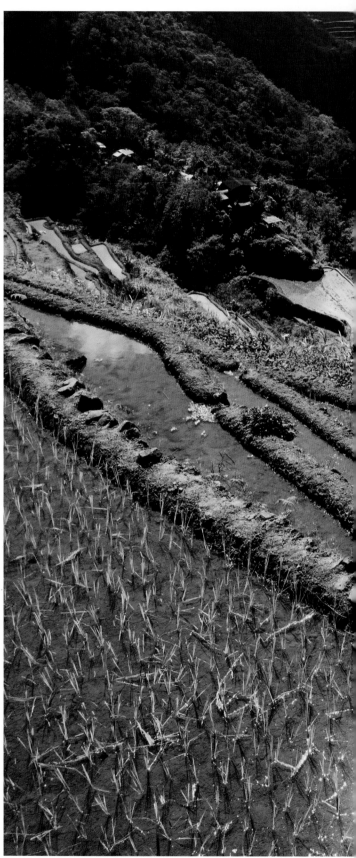

These pages: Humankind has impacted upon the Cordillera Central mountains of northern Luzon for many years. One of the grandest and earliest examples is the huge rice terracing sculpted into the mountains around Banaue, and particularly at the nearby village of Batad (right), built about 2000 years ago, and today a UNESCO World Heritage Site. At the end of the rainy season, in early spring, vibrantly green rice plants that have been germinated in nurseries are bundled up and planted out across the terraces, a process that has been repeated time and again since these terraces were carved out of the mountains (above).

These pages: Though generally not well known for its beaches, Luzon's coast is nevertheless quite varied and extremely beautiful. Sights range from the stunning forest-lined and very remote bay at Dimalansan (left), located on the northeast coast and protected within the huge Northern Sierra Madre Natural Park, to the highly visited limestone islands and coves of the Hundred Islands National Recreation Area (below, opposite below and opposite above right) on Luzon's much more accessible northwest coast. Fishing harbours are common, usually a lively scene crammed with quite an array of colourful *bancas*. For the visitor, one of the most important harbours in Luzon is Donsol (opposite above left), in the far south, from where it is possible at certain times of the year to take whale-shark watching trips.

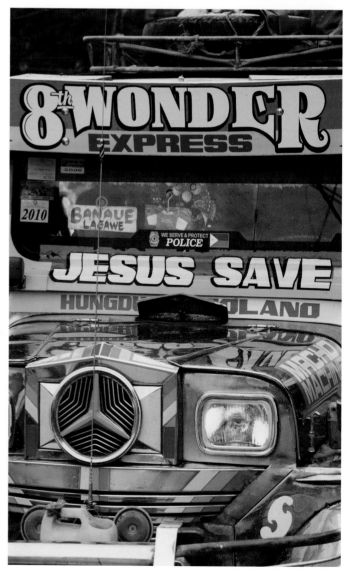

This page: The jeepney, the uniquely Filipino form of public transport, born years ago out of a lack of buses and an excess of American military jeeps, is like a canvas for a mass of pop-art, its expanses of shiny metal covered with luridly coloured slogans and drawings, often proclaiming the driver-owner's various allegiances. In urban areas the jeepney is used mainly for local transportation, but in the countryside can be used even for long distance journeys, despite their general lack of comfort.

Opposite page: Although much of Manila is renowned for being hugely overcrowded and poorly designed, there are areas of both classic and modern style. Perhaps most well known among these is the classically opulent Manila Hotel (opposite above left). There are also the sleek modern (if rather characterless) shopping malls, such as Robinson's Galleria (opposite above right), in Manila's Ermita district. More individual is the Greenbelt Park, an upmarket shopping centre that follows the path of a stream on its way through an otherwise concrete jungle (opposite below).

There is a diversity of architectural styles in the capital, Manila, from traditional to global modern. Many buildings in Intramuros were rebuilt following the destruction of the Second World War, including Manila Cathedral (above right) and a number of Hispanic-style buildings (below right). The traditional theme continues with the cool lushness of Paco Park, in Ermita (opposite above), and the opulent neo-classical fountains outside the Peninsula Hotel (opposite below right), in Makati. In contrast, ultra-modern glass and steel architecture is commonly seen throughout the commercial hub of Makati (above) and at the entrance to the Stock Exchange (opposite below left).

Opposite page: Luzon's landscapes are full of stunning tropical views, dominated by the deep intense greens of lush, vibrant vegetation and the vivid blues of water, indicative of the huge wealth of life and energy the warm, humid climate can generate. In an almost pristine environment, mangroves stand in the turquoise shallows of Triboa Bay, a forest-lined inlet of Subic Bay, and part of the Subic Watershed Forest Reserve (above). A tangle of vegetation fights for space and light on the forest floor at the foot of a tree, in the lowland rainforest that surrounds Bulusan volcano in Luzon's far south (below).

This page: Early morning mist wraps a swathe around the summit of Luzon's highest mountain, Mt Pulag (2930 m/9612 ft) centrepiece of Mt Pulag National Park. Dense stands of mossy rainforest cling to the steep slopes almost as far as the very summit, shortly below which the trees give way to an open area of grasses and dwarf bamboo (above). Rather differently, in Taal Volcano National Park, the view from the rim of the volcano's crater reveals a lake in which sits a tiny island (right). Amazingly, the entire volcano is surrounded by another lake, enclosed within a huge caldera. Despite the peaceful scene, Taal is rated as one of the Philippines' most dangerous volcanoes, overdue for a major eruption.

Chapter Seven

Palawan and Mindoro, the Wild Frontier

On the Philippines' westernmost fringes, the two island groups of Palawan and Mindoro are definitely the country's wild frontier and for the most part relatively thinly populated. Dense forests are still quite common, and both towns and roads are few and far between. Getting around requires patience, sometimes a little ingenuity, and from time to time a healthy sense of humour!

Opposite above: An islet just offshore from the lovely coast at Sabang, close to St Paul's Underground River National Park, on the west coast of Palawan.

Above: The stunning scarlet flowers of a Flame of the Forest tree, in El Nido town, Palawan.

Opposite below: A stream flows steeply down through dense, lush montane rainforest on the slopes of Mt Halcon, northeast Mindoro.

Left: A tree is lit by the golden light of sunset in Calauit Island Wildlife Sanctuary, with Calamian deer grazing in the distance; Calamian Islands, northern Palawan.

Palawan and Mindoro, the Wild Frontier

Palawan is a long, pencil-thin island plus a few other island clusters (principally the Calamian Islands to the north). Though rugged, the terrain is mostly relatively low-lying, even its mountains quite small by Philippine standards. It is the only part of the country to have ever had a land bridge to the rest of Southeast Asia, giving it a wildlife related to that of Malaysia and Indonesia.

Mindoro, on the other hand, is a roughly crescent-shaped island, its interior characterized by high mountains, the tallest 2587 m (8487 ft) Mt Halcon in the northeast and Mt Baco at 2487 m (8159 ft) in the south. Unfortunately, large-scale logging has ripped through Mindoro, causing immense environmental damage. Nevertheless, it is still home to a number of uniquely Philippine animal species, most famously the Tamaraw, a dwarf buffalo that inhabits the fringes of forest clearings. Badly hit by deforestation and hunting, it is teetering on the brink of extinction.

Along the coasts of both Mindoro and Palawan are some lovely coral reefs, though many have suffered considerable damage due to dynamite and cyanide usage. Most spectacular of all is Tubbataha Reef, a very remote atoll lying in the Sulu Sea, its island a nesting site for many sea birds, its waters home to a vast array of corals and fish, the latter ranging from tiny reef fish to sharks and manta rays.

Both island groups have experienced considerable immigration from other parts of the Philippines. On Mindoro most newcomers have settled in and around the towns along the east coast, while in Palawan the focus has been around the provincial capital Puerto Princesa. Mindoro's native people, the Mangyan, are a very poor farming community, living in small, remote villages. Badly hit by logging, they have become highly suspicious of outsiders and are reluctant to cooperate in efforts to conserve the remaining forests. They are now blamed for continuing environmental damage caused by slash-and-burn farming methods.

Palawan is home to a number of cultural minorities, most especially the Tagbanua, a shy group of farmers living mainly in the Calamian Islands of the north, and the Pala'wan, living in the hills and forests of the south. The Badjao, or Sea Gypsies, are scattered along the coast of much of Palawan, living mainly in houses built on stilts over the water.

For the visitor, the natural environment is the big attraction. For divers and beach-lovers, the most accessible location is Puerto Galera, a collection of beaches and resorts at the northern tip of Mindoro. Here the coral reefs have been protected over many years, creating some stunning diving and snorkelling sites. Tubbataha Reef is the ultimate goal for the serious diver, a site reachable only by live-aboard dive boat, operating only in April and May.

El Nido is arguably Palawan's most famous attraction, its spectacular Bacuit Bay and Archipelago a fabulous collection of beaches, islands and karst limestone cliffs. Coming a very close second to El Nido is the St Paul's Underground River National Park, a UNESCO World Heritage Site near Puerto Princesa. Here, a river flowing through a limestone cave before emptying onto the beach, can be explored by boat.

For the serious hiker, Mindoro's mountains are the ultimate challenge. These are real wilderness experiences, and should not be attempted alone – for Mt Halcon at least, guides can be hired in the nearby town of Calapan. They are also extremely rainy places, receiving many thousands of millimetres a year, with heavy rainfall an almost daily occurrence. For this reason, it is not really safe to attempt a climb outside the drier months of April and May.

Opposite above left: The lovely pink flower of the kapok tree, cultivated by the Tagbanua people on Coron Island. Its fluffy seeds are used for stuffing pillows and cushions.

Opposite above right: A Puffer fish hides in one of the thousands of crevasses typical of a coral reef, and which make them such a perfect habitat for many fish.

Opposite right: Sunlight pours down onto the trunk of a large tree, draped with lianas, in lowland rainforest on Langen Island, one of the many islands in Bacuit Bay, El Nido, Palawan.

This page: Located in a remote part of northern Palawan, El Nido is undoubtedly one of the most beautiful and exotic of the Philippines' resort areas, the sheltered Bacuit Bay littered with a mass of spectacular karst limestone islands. Bungalows of the deluxe Lagen Island Resort stand on their own private island, surrounded by a thickly vegetated garden, and on the edge of dense rainforest (top left and centre left). In this almost roadless area, boats are the ubiquitous mode of transport, so keeping them well-maintained, like this boat pulled up onto the beach on the edge of El Nido town, is essential (below left). At dusk Cadlao Island, one of the largest islands in Bacuit Bay, makes a stunning silhouette when seen from the harbour at El Nido town (above).

This page: St Paul's Underground River National Park, a UNESCO World Heritage Site, where a river flows through a vast limestone cave, is one of Palawan's most visited attractions, relatively close to the provincial capital, Puerto Princesa. It is quite straightforward to explore part of the cave in a paddled canoe, park staff organizing regular trips in their boats, setting out from the beach-side lagoon (top and above). As soon as the river flows out of its cave, it empties into a coastal lagoon, surrounded by mangroves and palm trees, and separated from the sea by a sandy beach (left). From here the water then drains into the sea.

This page: Although some of the more accessible reefs have been damaged, Palawan's submarine world is still a stunningly beautiful and highly varied environment teeming with some of the world's most beautiful aquatic life. A turtle cruises effortlessly across coral reef shallows, close to Bird Islet, at the northern end of Tubbataha Reef National Marine Park (top left). Bigeye Trevally *(Caranx sexfasciatus)* commonly swim in large shoals across reefs that are adjacent to deep water (centre left). The spectacular Lionfish *(Pterois volitans)*, equipped with poisonous spines and adorned with elaborate fins, is ubiquitous to reefs all over the Philippines (left). A diver moves in on one of the wartime wrecks of Coron Bay, a popular attraction for divers. Though the water here is quite murky, the wrecks have become superb artificial reefs, harbouring an assortment of marine life (above).

This page: A spectacluar inlet filled with turquoise water and surrounded by sheer karst limestone cliffs, a typical view along the coast of Coron Island, one of the Calamian Islands of northern Palawan. Although stunningly beautiful and only a relatively short boat ride from the town of Coron on neighbouring Busuanga Island, the island remains unspoilt and lightly visited due to the shyness and protective tendencies of the Tagbanua people who live here. The Tagbanua lead a mostly subsistence fishing and farming lifestyle (above). The vivid red of a *Dendronephthya* species soft tree coral always takes centre stage even in any vibrant coral reef, seen here at El Nido (left).

Opposite page: The coral atoll of Tubbataha Reef, in the midst of the Sulu Sea, is very remote. As a result it still teems with wildlife, and is a must for keen divers. Japanese divers prepare for an early morning dive (far left). The beach and vegetation along the shore of Bird Islet, a major bird-nesting ground at the reef's northern end (left). A diver hovers behind a sea fan on the reef wall (below left).

This page: Much of Tubbataha Reef consists of a dense jumble of a huge diversity of corals (below). Tubbataha is one of the few places in the Philippines where Manta Rays, *Manta birostris*, are commonly seen (right). A Tawny Nurse shark, *Nebrius ferrugineus*, rests in the shelter of a cave (centre right). The Napoleon Wrasse, *Cheilinus undulatus*, is one of the most spectacular of Tubbataha's fish (below right).

This page: Palawan's plant and animal wildlife is immensely varied, but rather different from that of the rest of the Philippines, being more closely related to the wildlife of mainland Southeast Asia. The Hill Mynah, *Gracula religiosa*, popular for its renowned ability to talk, is still widespread but is under great pressure due to hunting for the pet trade (top). A monitor lizard, *Varanus* species, a very common reptile in St Paul's Underground River National Park, scurries across the park's forest floor (above). Brown Boobies, *Sula leucogaster*, resting on Bird Islet, Tubbataha Reef National Marine Park. This large gannet is common across the Pacific and in the Philippines is frequently seen around the Sulu Sea (above right). Scattered mangrove trees, outliers of a large, dense mangrove forest nearby, line the shore of Calauit Island Wildlife Sanctuary, an extremely remote island in the northwest of the Calamian group, northern Palawan (right).

This page: Long-tailed, or Crab-eating macaques, *Macaca fascicularis*, are common in Palawan's forests, seen here at St Paul's Underground River National Park (top left). The Saltwater Crocodile, *Crocodylus porosus*, is widespread from northern Australia, through Southeast Asia to India, but is seriously endangered in many areas. The Philippine population is believed to be quite small. The crocodile here was protected within the Calauit Island Wildlife Sanctuary, in the far north of Palawan (top right). A wild tortoise hides among the dry leaf litter on the forest floor on Coron Island. Although endangered across Palawan, these tortoises have a reasonably safe home on Coron Island, due to the low population and the local Tagbanua people's generally gentle nature (above).

This page: Palawan's mostly rural population live very close to nature, dependent on its products for their livelihoods, while tourists come to get a taste of its natural beauty. Watched by her children, a Tagbanua woman on Coron Island cleans material extracted from swifts' nests, the basis for bird's nest soup and the source of much of the Coron people's income (centre left). For visitors, the islands and beaches of Bacuit Bay are a major attraction, accessible only by boat, ranging from the lightly visited and pristine beach on Dolbaduen Island (above left), to the much more accessible Commando Beach, close to El Nido town (above and bottom left).

Opposite page: Sabang is well known as the only access point for St Paul's Underground River National Park, while its stunning beach has largely escaped development (above). The beautiful natural harbour at El Nido town is home to a large fleet of *bancas*, some used for fishing, others for ferrying visitors to island resorts around Bacuit Bay (below).

This page: Mt Halcon, Mindoro's highest mountain, is a wild, rugged and remote place. During a respite from frequent rain, it is possible, from a vantage point at about 1000 m (3300 ft), to see across Halcon's main massif towards the summit (top). The Tamaraw, *Bubalus mindorensis*, is a highly endangered dwarf buffalo that survives only on Mindoro, where it inhabits forest fringes (above). Slash-and-burn farming by the local Mangyan people destroys large amounts of forest on Mindoro every year, as seen here on Mt Halcon's lower slopes (right), but it is an essential part of their subsistence farming.

This page: A dense tangle of vegetation in montane rainforest on Halcon's middle slopes (above). The spectacular flower of the shrub *Medinilla magnifica*, seen here in forest on Mt Halcon, is unfortunately increasingly rare due to loss of habitat (above right). Orchids are a common sight in Philippine forests, and Mt Halcon is particularly well endowed with a wide variety of unusual species, particularly in the montane forests (right).

This page: The coral atoll of Apo Reef Marine Natural Park is one of the remotest parts of Mindoro, lying between its west coast and the northeast shores of Palawan's Calamian Islands. Much of the atoll's island is a sandy beach, where turtles nest and driftwood is washed ashore (top). The water across the atoll is very shallow, with a sandy bottom, making for some spectacular turquoise waters (right). More accessible is the resort of Puerto Galera, at Mindoro's northern tip, a peninsula with a string of beautiful beaches and well-protected coral reefs. It also has a large natural harbour, at the entrance to which is a sandy promontory backed by a forest of coconut palms (top right). The resort's beaches are typically overhung with trees, usually the ubiquitous coconut, but often unique beach forest trees, including the *Barringtonia*, which every day at sunrise drops its delicate and stunningly beautiful flowers onto the sand (above).

This page: With few roads linking up the beaches and villages of the Puerto Galera peninsula, boats are the main way to get around, the *bancas* either working as ferries between beaches or providing sightseeing, diving and snorkelling tours. Every beach is lined with quite an extensive fleet of boats, such as that seen here at Small La Laguna Beach (left and below).

This page: The stunning underwater world of Palawan and Mindoro. A Green Turtle, *Chelonia mydas*, cruises across coral in Bacuit Bay, El Nido, still an important turtle nesting area, and one of the easiest places in the Philippines for divers and snorkellers to see this reptile (above). In the waters around Puerto Galera, feeding fish is a popular activity for divers. So common has it become that the fish expect it, typically crowding around divers before any food is even offered (left).

Opposite page: A *Xestospongia* species barrel sponge, arguably the largest, most spectacular and most easily recognized of the Philippines' many sponge species, sits among corals off Puerto Galera (top). A cluster of *Xenia* species soft corals off Puerto Galera (below left). Detail of a bright scarlet *Acalycigorgia* species sea fan, Apo Reef Marine Natural Park, Mindoro (below right).

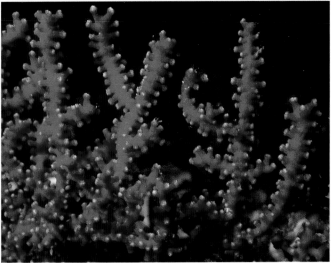

Chapter Eight

The Visayas, Island and Beach Life

If the word 'Philippines' conjures up images of blindingly white sandy beaches, sparkling azure water and a life spent lazily chugging from island to island in a brightly painted outrigger boat, then you are thinking of the Visayas. There can be little doubt that this mass of islands making up the fragmented centre of the Philippine archipelago is the main attraction for visitors, mostly for the region's stunning beaches and coral reefs, as well as some of its smaller, beach-ringed islands, the quintessential tropical island paradises.

Above left: Beautifully painted *paraw*, or sailing *bancas*, used as working fishing boats, drawn up on the beach at Miagao, near Iloilo, Panay.

Above: Children collecting sea shells on one of the many stunning beaches on Boracay Island, Panay.

Opposite below: Shoreline coconut palms silhouetted against the sunrise, at Alona Beach, Panglao Island, Bohol.

Left: Alocasia, or wild yams, growing in dense montane rainforest on Mt Talinis, Southern Negros Forest Reserve, near Dumaguete, Negros.

The Visayas, Island and Beach Life

The Visayas do not consist merely of beach-strewn islands, of course. The main islands of Panay, Negros, Bohol, Cebu, Samar and Leyte collectively constitute a considerable land area, with Cebu home to the country's second city and economic power house, Cebu City. The region generally is of major economic importance, site of several copper and gold mines, as well as producing a number of vital agricultural crops, especially sugar cane and coconuts. Population pressure is high here, resulting in significant outward migration to such areas as Palawan and Mindoro.

Inevitably, the islands' once lush rainforests have been heavily plundered and on Cebu, for example, only pockets of forest now survive. However, a number of forested areas do remain, such as on Negros' Mt Kanlaon, in the mountains of western Panay, across central Bohol, and most especially on the less densely settled islands of Samar and Leyte. The forests of these last two islands are home to a small number of the endangered Philippine Eagle.

Over-fishing – often involving the use of dynamite and cyanide – and deforestation have all had a seriously damaging effect on many of the region's coral reefs and their fish populations. However, it is hoped that the many small scale conservation efforts now in place will over time help to restore many of those reefs. Increasing numbers of fishing communities have been encouraged to set up their own no-fishing reserves on local reefs, steps that have been found to have a remarkably rapid effect on fish stocks, increasing fish numbers in neighbouring fishing areas, benefitting both the environment and the fishermen.

For the visitor, there is no doubt that the region's main draws are its stunningly white coral sand beaches and those coral reefs which are still in good condition. The country's number one tourist attraction, the spectacularly beautiful Boracay Island, lies off the northern coast of Panay. A tiny dot of land, Boracay is famed for its magnificent White Beach, stretching about 3 km (1.8 miles) along its west coast, although it also has numerous other lovely beaches. Such is the great length of White Beach that it has easily been able to absorb the steadily increasing numbers of visitors without appearing at all crowded. Throughout much of its tourist history – which started in the 1980s – its development has been very simple and low key, but with new deluxe hotel, apartment and golf course developments taking place there is a growing danger of over-development. Another great beach resort is the south coast of Panglao Island, part of Bohol, and in particular Alona Beach and the nearby Balicasag Island.

Well preserved coral reefs exist close to both of these beach areas, particularly around Balicasag. This tiny island is surrounded by deep waters, so its fringing reef attracts a vast array of fish from little, colourful butterfly fish, to huge groupers and vast shoals of barracuda and tuna. Another superb diving resort is Moalboal on the southwest coast of Cebu. Here, coral reefs along the mainland shore and surrounding the nearby islet of Pescador, are in pristine condition, and also being surrounded by deep water attract a vast array of fish. The region's waters are also good for spotting dolphins and whales, the former readily seen in the Tanon Strait separating Negros and Cebu, the latter around the island of Pamilacan, off the south coast of Bohol.

Inland attractions include Bohol's Chocolate Hills, an expanse of small, perfectly rounded hills, attractively green much of the year but a chocolate brown during the dry season. On Negros stands the Visayas' tallest mountain, Mt Kanlaon (2465 m/8085 ft), presenting a challenging hike through dense rainforest. An active volcano, the mountain is topped by an awesome crater as well as stunning all-round views. Always hike with a guide and climb Kanlaon only when there are no eruption warnings.

Opposite above left: With so many islands, life in the Visayas inevitably revolves around the sea. Fishermen sort through a new catch, just brought ashore, on the beach at Miagao, near Iloilo, Panay.
Opposite above right: Tiny Apo Island, off the southern tip of Negros, is a mecca for divers, who brave its fierce currents to see its superb corals, sponges and fish shoals.
Opposite: Sandy beaches abound, the most famous among them the stunning White Beach, on Boracay Island, Panay.

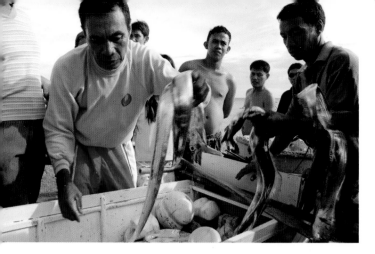

This page: With its stunning beaches, the small island of Boracay, off the northern tip of Panay, is justifiably the Philippines' number one attraction for overseas visitors. Although White Beach is the main attraction, other beaches and resort areas are popular, including Diniwid, just north of White Beach (above). During the heat of the day, quite a few visitors opt to take it easy beneath beach umbrellas and coconut palms (right).

This page: Being a busy tourist resort, Boracay has all the facilities a visitor needs, though mostly rather low key and low rise – at least along White Beach – helping to produce a laidback ambience. Although the hotels are mostly modern and well equipped, many aim to retain a rustic feel, such as at Friday's Resort (top). Beachside restaurants and bars, too, frequently make use of thatch and bamboo to maintain the rural atmosphere (left and below right).

These pages: One of the great attractions of Boracay, and particularly White Beach, is the huge number of colourful *paraw*, or sailing *bancas*, that line the shore. While in the past many were used for local fishing, today the majority are used for hired trips around the island and to more remote beaches. A view along the northern end of White Beach shows quite a busy scene, not only of sunbathers but also of a cluster of *paraw* preparing for tours (below). These boats' incredibly shallow draught – enabled by the stabilizing effect of the outriggers – makes it possible for the boatmen to haul their craft right up onto the beach, where they can wait for customers (right and opposite).

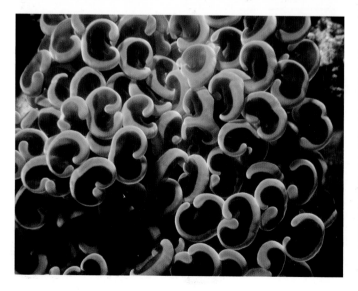

Opposite page: Where reefs are healthy, the Visayas' submarine environment is wonderfully colourful and diverse. Polyps of *Xenia* species soft corals crowd together, Balicasag Island, Bohol (above right). The polyps of egg-like Bubble coral, *Plerogyra* species, usually form hemispherical colonies, as here off Boracay (above left). Growing like bunches of grapes on stems, this *Oxycorynia* species sea squirt or tunicate is only occasionally seen on Philippine reefs, here found off Boracay (centre left). The anchor-shaped ends to the tentacles of *Euphyllia ancora* make it superficially resemble a bubble coral; Boracay (below left). The beautiful lattices of the sea fans, which may be up to a couple of metres across, are commonly seen on the deeper parts of a reef. Usually brightly coloured, they are only occasionally white. This *Acabaria* species was seen off Balicasag Island, Bohol (below right).

This page: A shoal of jacks swimming in deep water close to the reef surrounding Apo Island, Negros (right). A colourful diversity of hard and soft corals, Danjugan Island, Negros (below).

These pages: The beaches of Panglao Island, off the southwestern tip of Bohol, are among the most lovely and popular in the Visayas. Both the sand and coconut palms at Alona Beach seem to glow in the golden light of sunrise (left). Just after sunrise, a young boy pauses in his cycling along Alona Beach (top). A diving boat sits on its mooring just offshore from Alona Beach, lit by the warm rays of sunset (above).

These pages: Although Alona Beach, on the south coast of Panglao Island, is a great place to just relax it is also a perfect base for trips out to nearby Balicasag Island, one of the Philippines' top diving sites. Partially hidden by a coconut palm hanging over Alona beach, a dive boat sits on its mooring in readiness for an afternoon diving session (left). Bancas lie on a sandy beach, on the edge of the beautiful azure sea that surrounds Balicasag Island (opposite). From a distance Balicasag is just a totally flat, though forested, sand-ringed island (top). In the evening, Alona Beach turns into a series of open-air restaurants, tables laid out on the sand (top), freshly caught seafood laid out on ice ready for diners (above).

This page: The bird life of the Visayas region is wonderfully colourful and diverse, some species are endemic to the Philippines, others are found across Southeast Asia. The Pink-necked Green Pigeon, *Treron vernans*, is quite widespread, often seen in coastal scrub and mangroves (above left). The Black-naped Oriole, *Oriolus chinensis*, is common across the Philippines, found in open country, orchards and gardens (centre left). Unique to the Philippines, the Blue-naped Parrot, *Tanygnathus lucionensis*, has become quite rare due to trapping for the pet trade (below left). The White-throated Kingfisher, *Halcyon smyrnensis*, is quite common across much of Southeast Asia, and is frequently seen in the Philippines on farmlands and in forest edges (below).

This page: The Tarictic Hornbill, *Penelopides panini*, one of the Philippines' endemic hornbills, is dependent on healthy rainforest, where it feeds on fruiting trees. It exists as several races, some of which are close to extinction (above). Another Philippine endemic species is the Blue-crowned Racquet-tail, *Prioniturus discurus*, which also lives in the forests feeding on fruiting trees (above right). A widespread and common bird is the Pompadour Green-pigeon, *Treron pompadora*, which – despite being so common – is actually very hard to see due to its excellent camouflage green colouring (centre right). The Asiatic Grass Owl, *Tyto capensis*, is widespread thoughout Southeast Asia, including the Philippines, where it lives from sea level up to quite high in the mountains (below right).

Opposite page: Bohol is an intensely rural island, quite thinly populated by Philippine standards. When not working, buffalo are left to graze, as seen here at Loboc in Bohol's south, often accompanied by cattle egrets (above left). In the village of Loboc many houses and their gardens are adorned with colourful orchids (above right). On the south coast, close to the village of Loay, is a huge marsh composed largely of Nipa palms, used extensively for thatch roofs and walls (below).

This page: One of the Philippines' most famous landscape views is the Chocolate Hills, a collection of rounded hills in central Bohol (right). Some way to the south runs the lovely Loboc River, its banks crowded with a verdant cloak of trees and palms, seen here at the village of Loboc (below).

This page: Philippine festivals are raucous, energetic and friendly affairs that the local people throw themselves into enthusiastically, none more so than in the Visayas. Dinagyang Festival, held each January in Iloilo, Panay, is one of the biggest and most organized. A major part of the festival is for dance troupes to perform elaborate and highly choreographed dances in two extremely competitive contests. In the first, the *Kasadyahan*, troupes perform a wide range of dance types and wear equally diverse costumes, ranging from traditional rural Philippine to traditional Spanish (right and top right). In the second and more popular dance competition, the *Ati-Atihan*, dancers wear tribal-type costumes, with skin blackened to recall the aboriginal Aeta people that used to live throughout this region (top). Outside the main dance arenas, the streets of Iloilo are crammed with people and snack stalls, and much of the city centre is closed off to traffic (above).

This page: Some of the Dinagyang dance costumes are truly imaginative, none more so than this ensemble of children dressed as crabs (above). Festival souvenirs are widely available at streetside stalls, most notable being these miniature Ati-Atihan masks (top). The Ati-Atihan Festival held each January in Kalibo, northern Panay, is just as spectacular as Iloilo's Dinagyang, but much less controlled, with the crowds of spectators able to merge with the participants on the streets. The main day starts with a colourful procession of participating teams (above right). This is followed by troupes, usually from schools, villages or sports teams, performing dances in a range of magnificent costumes. The dances are usually less energetic or extensively choreographed, at least partly because so many spectators are able to mingle with the participants (centre right and below right)!

This page: Cebu City is a mix of some of the Philippines' oldest Spanish colonial and most modern international architecture. Perhaps oldest of all is Fort San Pedro, probably the Philippines' first permanent Spanish construction. Today, it survives as part of a lush green park (right and above right). Of immense historical importance is Cebu Cathedral (above), though it tends to live in the shadow of the much more famous and well-loved Santo Niño Basilica, home of the country's oldest Santo Niño statue.

This page: Although many churches date from the Spanish era, those of the home-grown Iglesia ni Cristo sect are stunning modern structures of soaring spires and sweeping arches. The one in Cebu City is typical (above). The modern part of Cebu City consists of well-ordered buildings, separated by wide boulevards that are able to cope with the huge amount of traffic (above right). The old part of the city, near the port and sea front, though rather ramshackle and crowded, is still a major commercial hub, site of the huge Carbon Market, where it is possible to buy an enormous diversity of goods, of which dried foods and flowers are just two (centre and below right).

This page: Dumaguete is a pleasant university city on the coast of southern Negros. In the city centre lies Rizal Park, a tree-shaded oasis that screens out the bustle of the streets (above). To the south lies Malatapay, site of a weekly market that brings in people and farm produce from far and wide (top). Penetrating the forested mountains of the nearby Southern Negros Forest Reserve area can be tricky, frequent rains bringing landslides down onto the only motorable track (above left). Across the Tanon Strait from Dumaguete, on the west coast of Cebu, lies Moalboal, a mecca for divers due to the nearby pristine coral reefs. Motor tricycle is the usual way to get around Moalboal, particularly to reach nearby Panagsama Beach, site of the divers' lodges (left).

Opposite page: Most of Panagsama Beach is rocky, but there are some sandy stretches, backed by vibrant bourgainvillea (above). The Tanon Strait, seen here from Moalboal, is an extremely deep stretch of water separating Cebu from Negros (below).

These pages: Sohoton National Park is a place of deep limestone gorges and caves, carved by the rivers that pour down from the forest in this area, hidden in a remote corner of southern Samar. The only way to reach the park is by a long boat ride up the Cadacan River from the coastal village of Basey (top). Upon arrival at the park, boats pull into a lagoon in an enormous limestone amphitheatre, right next to the cave entrances (above left and left). Park rangers will show visitors around the most accessible cave, the Panhulugan I Cave, a stunning series of chambers lined with glistening stalactites and stalagmites (above and opposite).

These pages: From coast to mountain, Negros is a rugged but verdant place, attractive to visitors with a love of outdoor adventure. Apo Island, off Negros' southern tip is an exciting dive site, though its beach serves mainly as a working fishing harbour for the island's residents (above left). The fishing life can be a hard one, many fishermen living in poverty, as attested by this beachside family home at Dauin (centre left). A spine of high mountains runs along much of the island's length, parts densely forested and site of many spectacular waterfalls, such as Pulang Tubig in the north of the island (above). Towering over Negros is Mt Kanlaon, at 2465 m (8085 ft) the Visayas' highest mountain and a very active volcano. Much of it is cloaked in dense forest that can be hard work to hike through (below left) but once near the summit the views are stunning (opposite below). The active crater is a vast menacing chasm that erupts fairly frequently (opposite above).

Chapter Nine

Mindanao and the Islamic South

It has to be said that the name 'Mindanao' seems to be synonymous with trouble, parts of the island having been subjected to civil strife in the name of one cause or another off and on over the past 100 years. Today, troubles still continue, but only in limited pockets of the region and only sporadically. Much of Mindanao is perfectly peaceful and safe, and in recent years has been increasingly opened up to visitors.

Opposite above: A glorious sunset over the harbour at Zamboanga, near the western tip of Mindanao.

Above: A Collared Kingfisher, *Halcyon chloris*, a very common coastal bird, seen in mangroves on Siargao Island, northeast Mindanao.

Opposite below: A lone coconut palm leans across the sands of Guyam Islet, off the coast of Siargao Island.

Left: A line of *vintas*, *paraws* with brightly coloured sails, a well known feature of Zamboanga.

Mindanao and the Islamic South

Second largest of the Philippines' islands, much of Mindanao is quite mountainous, while two very low-lying areas in the northeast and south have created huge swamps. The eastern part of the island has the highest mountains, including the country's two highest peaks, Mt Apo at 2954 m (9691 ft) and Mt Dulang-Dulang which is 2938 m high (9639 ft), the latter the highest peak in the Mt Kitanglad range. Until comparatively recently, the prolonged troubles helped to keep the loggers away, ensuring that significant parts of the mountains are still well forested, creating the country's most extensive home for the endangered Philippine Eagle. However, agricultural pressures are high, much of the high plateau east of Mt Dulang-Dulang, for example, having been converted to a huge expanse of pineapple plantations.

As usual in the Philippines, a number of lesser islands lie scattered around the coast of the main island. In the north are Camiguin and the Siargao group, both popular with visitors, while to the southwest, and running as a long island chain that reaches as far as Borneo, is the Sulu archipelago. Sulu is the heartland of Islamic Philippines, the area first converting to Islam in the 14th and 15th centuries, home of the country's first Islamic sultanate, created in 1457. Nowadays it is part of the self-governing Autonomous Region in Muslim Mindanao (ARMM).

Although much of Mindanao's countryside is not densely populated, the island is site of several large cities, most notably Davao City, the country's third city, plus General Santos, Cagayan de Oro, Iligan, Cotabato and Zamboanga. These cities are largely non-Muslim, the product of immigration from other parts of the Philippines. Despite this immigration, Mindanao is still home to a wide assortment of cultural minority groups, both Moslem and non-Moslem.

The Islamic groups are, not surprisingly, concentrated in the west and southwest, and include the Tausug and Badjao mostly in Sulu, the Maranao around Lake Lanao, the Yakan of Basilan island and the Maguindanao of Maguindanao province. Mindanao's non-Islamic groups, collectively known as Lumad, mostly continue to practise animist religious beliefs, and are scattered across much of Mindanao. They include the Manobo, Tasaday and Mandaya in the east, and the T'boli of central southern Mindanao.

For the visitor, the main attractions lie in the east and north of Mindanao. Off the northeast coast, the Siargao Islands have become a surfers' Mecca due to the huge surf breaks occurring along their eastern shore. More recently, the islands have also started to become popular for diving and sea angling. A little further west and off Mindanao's north coast is the lovely teardrop-shaped Camiguin Island. On this beautiful and friendly island the main visitor activity is chilling out on the volcanic grey sand beaches, though for those needing a break from this there is some diving, a hot spring to soak in and some hiking to be done. The island is very mountainous, dominated by five volcanoes, one of which, Mt Hibok-Hibok, is active. It can be climbed in a day.

Further south, close to Davao City, the Philippine Eagle Foundation has its headquarters. Set in a lovely park northwest of the city, not only can this huge eagle be seen here, but also a number of the Philippines' other birds of prey, such as the Philippine Hawk-Eagle and the Brahminy Kite. More hiking is available at the nearby Mt Apo, a two-day return hike from the road head at Lake Agco. Always take a guide, and first pick up a permit at the tourism council's office in Kidapawan. For beach life in the south, head to Samal Island, just east of Davao City.

Opposite above left: One of the world's most endangered species is the extremely rare Sulu Hornbill, *Anthracoceros montani*, always endemic to the Sulu Islands but now believed to be restricted to just one island in the group, Tawi-Tawi.

Opposite above right: There is a huge diversity of orchids, both wild and cultivated varieties, the latter frequently seen adorning village gardens.

Opposite below: Some of the Philippines' wildest forests survive in the mountains of central Mindanao, forming the main stronghold for the Philippine Eagle, one of the country's emblems. Naturally, trees within the forest vary greatly in size, the largest standing head and shoulders above the forest canopy, as in this image of a tree silhouetted against the sunrise.

These pages: Camiguin is a fabulously verdant island, lightly visited and tied very much to the rhythms of fishing and farming. Fishing boats line most of its volcanic black sand beaches, many going out to work either overnight or in the early morning (opposite), using mainly handlines but occasionally immense bamboo fish traps (opposite above left). Farming is less important, much of the land being far too steep for cultivation. However, some areas between the sea and the mountains have been converted to rice fields, particularly along the east coast (right). Tourism is still quite small, but the main attraction is undoubtedly White Island, a white sand bar that lies off the island's northern tip (opposite above right). Inland, and arguably more spectacular than White Island, is the magnificent Katibawasan Falls, a vertical ribbon of water set in a forested park that attracts mostly locals (above). Hotels lie scattered along Camiguin's coast, one of the most long-established of which is Caves Dive Resort, at Agoho, near the island's northern tip (above right).

These pages: The Siargao Islands, off Mindanao's northeast coast, are a remote archipelago where life still follows very traditional rhythms in both work and religion. Fishing is inevitably a mainstay, with every family member, including children usually taking part, as in this image of a family working a seine net cast off a beach from Guyam islet (opposite). At festival time, people from the outer islands bring their religious icons across in boats to be blessed at the main island's church in the town of General Luna (left and below).

This page: Population pressure is relatively low on the Siargao Islands, leading the natural environment to be in generally good health, a reasonable balance existing between nature and the needs of the islanders. As a result, the entire island group has become a protected area. The harbour at General Luna, one of the main towns, is little more than a sandy beach backed by dense coconut groves (right). Nearby, much of the sheltered shore is lined with beach forest and mangroves, a valuable habitat for wildlife (below).

This page: Offshore reefs ensure that even the east coast of the main island, otherwise exposed to the Pacific Ocean, is quite sheltered. A particularly quiet evening leaves the water mirror calm in a cove at Cloud Nine, a well known surfing spot (top left). Much of the west coast consists of a vast mangrove and nipa palm swamp, still home to crocodiles, though parts have been opened up to give boat access to the town of Del Carmen (top right). Working in the swamp, harvesting the nipa palms and laying fish and crab traps, is hard and poorly paid work, residents living mainly in simple wood and nipa palm huts (above). Not all is totally well with Siargao's environment, as the skeleton of a lone, dead mangrove tree testifies, all that remains of a mangrove forest cut down for firewood (left).

This page: The mainland of Mindanao is well known for its rugged terrain, much of it still forested, with just a few beach resorts along its coastline. Perhaps the most well known of its beaches is at Dakak Park, near Dipolog on the north coast (above). Central Mindanao is a land of high mountains and dense forests, nowhere more so than in the Mt Kitanglad range, the Philippines' second highest mountain (right). Here, vegetation is mostly deep green, but there are occasional vividly coloured forest flowers, such as this lovely pink *Impatiens* species bloom (above right).

This page: Rivers draining the mountains flow down into deep, low-lying valley areas, where – in at least two major parts of Mindanao – the land is so close to sea level that water flow becomes sluggish, resulting in huge marshes. In eastern Mindanao lies Agusan Marsh, extending along much of the Agusan River valley. Here life is adapted to being flooded for much of the year, with specialized swamp forest and rafts of purple-flowering water hyacinth (above). Even here, people make their home, mostly the Manobo group, who live their lives in villages either built on stilts or floating on rafts (top right and centre right), and whose only means of transport is by boat (below right).

Opposite page: Mt Apo is the Philippines' highest mountain, reaching 2954 m (9691 ft) and lying southwest of Davao. A volcanic mountain, it has several hot springs and is the site of a geothermal power station. Long protected as a national park, much of the mountain is still well forested, a stronghold of the Philippine Eagle. One of the best views of the summit is from the shore of Lake Venado (below). From the summit itself, there are stunning views, such as across some of the mountain's lower slopes, where some forest restoration work has been carried out (above).

This page: Flowing down Apo's northwest slopes is the Marbel River, which has to be forded repeatedly during the hike to the summit (above). Near the village of Ilomavis, the starting point for one of the main mountain trails, lies Lake Agco, a steaming geothermal lake (above right). On Apo's middle slopes, in dense montane rainforest, you'll come across large numbers of these incredible pandanus trees (right).

This page: Like the rest of the Philippines', Mindanao's birdlife is colourful and varied, many species endemic just to this region. The Writhed Hornbill, *Aceros leucocephalus*, is a Mindanao endemic, dependent on healthy, undisturbed forest, and therefore increasingly endangered due to deforestation (above left). The Philippine Hawk-eagle, *Spizaetus philippensis*, is spread across the whole country (except Palawan), in Mindanao a common sight soaring above the forests (above). The Crested Serpent-eagle, *Spilornis cheela*, is spread across much of South and Southeast Asia, though the Philippines has its own distinct race, known as *holospilus*, found throughout the country in forests and plantations (left).

This page: The Philippine Eagle, *Pithecophaga jefferyi*, one of the world's largest birds of prey, is unique to the Philippines and highly endangered due to loss of its forest habitat, though parts of Mindanao remain a stronghold (above left). By contrast, the much smaller but equally distinctive Brahminy Kite, *Haliastur indus*, is widespread across much of Southeast Asia, as well as the Philippines (top). The Coleto, *Sarcops calvus*, is a type of mynah endemic to the Philippines and commonly seen in Mindanao's forests and plantations, made quite distinctive by the pink wattle on its head (above). The Rufous Hornbill, *Buceros hydrocorax*, is the Philippines' largest hornbill, divided into three distinct races endemic to different regions of the country. The image here shows the Mindanao race (left), distinguishable from the Luzon race, for example, by its whiter bill and cask (see p76 for comparison).

This page: A significant proportion of south and southwest Mindanao's population belongs to an assortment of cultural groups, both Moslem and Lumad, or non-Moslem. After Friday prayers, a Moslem woman and her children sit outside a Cotabato City mosque (above left). Children of the non-Moslem Kalagan tribe wearing traditional clothes, share a joke while in Cotabato City (top). A man of the Moslem Yakan group, dressed in handwoven traditional clothing, performs at a festival, Basilan Island (above). Manobo people, a tribe widespread across Mindanao, prepare for a ceremony in countryside near Kidapawan (left).

Opposite page: A Badjao, or Sea Gypsy, village, for these people typically built on stilts over the sea, here backed by the rugged limestone landscape of Tawi-Tawi Island.

This page: Southern Mindanao's cultural diversity and long-held traditions create a colurful mix of lifestyles and products. A woman of the T'boli group, one of the Lumad tribes, in traditional dress, South Cotabato (right). A handicraft market stall shows off a collection of T'boli textiles and brass vases (below).

Opposite page: Though still commonly used for fishing in daily life, a crowd of *vintas*, or *paraws* with colourful sails, take part in Zamboanga Festival (above left). At the opposite end of the fishing fleet, but barely less colourful, a group of fishing trawlers sit at their moorings in the port at Oroquieta City, in western Mindanao (above right). A stunningly colourful geometric pattern, typical of Islamic art, in a weaving by a Yakan woman, one of Mindanao's Moslem groups (below).

INDEX

Page numbers in **bold** represent images.